A "NEW AND IMPROVED" JESUS?

Sermons For Lent And Easter
Cycle C First Lesson Texts

BY BARBARA BROKHOFF

C.S.S Publishing Co., Inc.
Lima, Ohio

A "NEW AND IMPROVED" JESUS?

Copyright © 1991 by
The C.S.S. Publishing Company, Inc.
Lima, Ohio

All rights reserved. No part of this publication may be reproduced, stored in a retrieval system, or transmitted in any form or by any means, electronic, mechanical, photocopying, recording, or otherwise, without the prior permission of the publisher. Inquiries should be addressed to: The C.S.S. Publishing Company, Inc., 628 South Main Street, Lima, Ohio 45804.

Library of Congress Cataloging-in-Publication Data

Brokhoff, Barbara.
    A "new and improved" Jesus : sermons for Lent and Easter, Cycle C First Lesson texts / by Barbara Brokhoff.
       p.   cm.
    ISBN 1-55673-318-6
    1. Lenten sermons. 2. Holy-Week sermons. 3. Eastertide—Sermons.
4. Sermons, American. I. Title.
BV4277.B76 1991
252'.62—dc20   91-2776
                                                                                         CIP

9139 / ISBN 1-55673-318-6   PRINTED IN U.S.A.

This book is dedicated with love,
And to the Glory of God,
To Peg and Roy,
Bob and Ginny,
Betty —
and they will know the reason why!

— Barbara Brokhoff

Table Of Contents

Ash Wednesday   7
    Fasting In A Fast-food World
    Joel 2:1-2, 12-17a

Lent 1   13
    Are You A Basket Case?
    Deuteronomy 26:1-11

Lent 2   21
    The Problem With A Promise
    Genesis 15:1-12, 17-18

Lent 3   29
    A Fireside Chat
    Exodus 3:1-15

Lent 4   37
    Healing For The Past
    Joshua 5:9-12

Lent 5   47
    A "New And Improved" Jesus?
    Isaiah 43:16-21, 25

Passion/Palm Sunday   55
    Not "If" — But "How"?
    Isaiah 50:4-9a

Maundy Thursday   61
    Fresh Bread And New Wine
    Jeremiah 31:31-34

Good Friday   65
    The S & L That Didn't Fail!
    Isaiah 52:13—53:1-12

Easter 73
    Easter — Fact And Fiction!
    Acts 10:34-43

Easter 2 79
    Obedience Is An Ugly Word!
    Acts 5:27-32

Easter 3 89
    "Because Of You" Or "In Spite Of You?"
    Acts 9:1-20

Easter 4 99
    A Word Of Encouragement!
    Acts 13:15-16, 26-33, (38-39)

Easter 5 105
    Beware! Caution! Danger!
    Acts 14:8-18

Easter 6 113
    Grace Is An "Inside Job!"
    Acts 15:1-2, 11, 22-29

Ascension Sunday 121
    The "Ups And Downs" Of The Ascension
    Acts 1:1-11

Pentecost 131
    Death Of A Dream — Birth Of The Church
    Genesis 11:1-9 and Acts 2:1-4, 12

Ash Wednesday
Joel 2:1-2, 12-17a

Fasting In A Fast-food World

If I told you that I have a sure-fire, effortless plan whereby you can lose 25 pounds, with no exercise, and no money, would I have your attention? I thought so. You can't pick up a *Woman's Day* magazine, *Good Housekeeping, McCalls, Redbook, Ladies' Home Journal, Cosmopolitan, Reader's Digest*, or even the *National Enquirer* without finding at least one article on how to lose weight. It's a multi-million dollar business in America.

And, if you are overweight, you probably need to lose some fat to be more healthy. It's never easy, it takes a powerful lot of willpower and determination, it costs in effort, exercise, and dollars. Constantly we are urged to diet: diet to lose weight, diet to look better, diet to aid digestion, diet to build muscle, diet to control cholesterol, diet to lower blood pressure, diet to avoid heart attack. Sometimes the word that is used is not this ugly word "diet," but an even uglier one; "fasting."

A "healthy fast" is fine, but Ash Wednesday's text calls for a "holy fast." Fasting for the six weeks of Lent may, or may not, result in weight loss, but I can guarantee you it can result in a real gain of spiritual depth if properly followed.

I know this is asking a lot. We might be willing, even if it is difficult, to go on a "healthy fast" for the body, but would you even consider a "holy fast" for the soul?

Declare A Holy Fast

Our text is written in the Old Testament book of Joel. The prophet is calling the nation and people to repentance because the Day of the Lord is near. It is an appropriate message for this Ash Wednesday, the beginning of Lent. Lent comes from an old Anglo-Saxon word "to lengthen." It is nearing springtime and the days are getting longer as spring appears. But, for the Christian, for the church, Lent signals that party time is over, Mardi Gras is past, and now a whole new mood prevails. Once more we begin our annual, six-week pilgrimage to Good Friday's cross. We instinctively draw back, for words like repentance, fasting, discipline, and denial are hard words. But if we try to take shortcuts on the journey, or avoid responding to the call, we will never fully participate in the gladness and glory of Easter Day.

First, we hear the call of God, through the prophet Joel, to repent: repent of our sins, repent of our selfishness, repent of our thoughtlessness, repent of our neglect of the Word, repent of our failure to pray, repent of our neglect of God, repent of our failure to live up to the highest and best that we know. Oh, yes, we really need to repent! Only someone hopelessly hardened could say there was no need for us to repent.

One of the ways we give evidence of our true repentance is by fasting (Joel 2:12, 15). Weeping and fasting are outward signs of our genuine sorrow for sin. This "holy fasting" is to be an external expression in denying ourselves, and it is also to include a fasting and mourning of the heart. Until the heart is reached, every other act is just a meaningless formality and cold ritual. Our spiritual renewal must go far beyond just our outward activity, but at least it does begin there.

Fasting was a common practice in times of calamity and was intended to express the humility of the worshiper before the judgment of God. But "holy fasting" is not as popular as it once was. Our Catholic friends are no longer required by church ordinance to fast from meat on Fridays and during Lent. Protestants speak ever so piously in excusing themselves from fasting. They say, "Let's not take something from ourselves, let's add to our disciplines for Lent. Let's add more Bible reading, more prayer, more good deeds. That's far better than denying oneself."

These words sound good, and it's true that adding to our spiritual activities is worthy, and should be encouraged; but in reality this is usually a cop-out, a nice way to avoid "holy fasting." There is something in us humans that we don't like or want to deny the self anything it desires. Andrew Murray reminded us: "We have within us a self that has its poison from Satan — from hell — and yet we cherish and nourish it. What do we not do to please self and nourish self? We make the devil within us strong. Look at your own life. What are the works of hell? They are chiefly these three: self-will, self-trust, and self-exaltation."

Strange, isn't it, that religious fasting is so difficult for us? We all know of persons who for certain causes and political purposes have fasted. Prisoners in jail have often gone on strenuous fasts to obtain better living conditions. We will remember seeing vividly portrayed on television (May 1989) the 300 students falling in the streets of Beijing, China, as they fasted for political power and freedom.

And as we fast for health: we give up something if it reduces cholesterol, lets us live longer, or pleases us when we look in the mirror. But would we fast for God? Isn't that asking too much of a fast-food generation, a people that not only wants what we want to eat, but wants it now!

The fact is, it is very hard to have a "holy fast," to do it for God and for God alone. We'd much rather indulge ourselves. That's why gluttony is a deadly sin. The early desert fathers believed that a person's appetites are linked: full stomachs and jaded palates take the edge from our hunger and thirst for God. They spoil the appetite for righteousness. God grant that we may "hunger and thirst after righteousness" during these purple days of Lent, and rejoice in the privilege of a "holy fast" for Christ.

Center On God

If we are to engage in a "holy fast" during Lent, we need to remember that fasting must forever center on God, and God alone. If our fasting is not unto God, we have utterly failed. Our motives for fasting must never be for health benefits, for success in getting our prayers answered, for gaining new power. There is no motive high or holy enough to replace the desire for God as the center of our fasting.

John Wesley said, "Let fasting be done unto the Lord with our eye singly fixed on him. Let our intentions herein be this, and this alone, to glorify our Father which is in heaven."

So quickly, in our spiritual journey, do we find our motives mixed and our priorities confused. When *My Fair Lady* was having its long run on Broadway, a couple from Atlanta planned their whole vacation around the availability of tickets for a matinee performance. It was something like eight months in advance they had to secure their tickets.

They went to New York City on the proper weekend. They got to the theater in plenty of time, found their seats — they were good seats in the fourth row in the center section — took their seats, and settled down to enjoy the play. Every seat in the theater was filled except the seat to the left of the man. The curtain rose, and still no one had taken the seat. At intermission, he turned to the woman on the opposite side of the empty seat and said, "This is amazing! We had to buy our tickets eight months in advance, and we get here and find an empty seat."

She said, "Well, that seat belongs to me, too. It was my husband's seat. He died." The man replied, "I'm terribly sorry. But couldn't you have invited a friend to come with you?" She answered, "No, they were all at the funeral."

So it is, one of the first things to happen when we try to center on God is that our priorities are found to be topsy-turvy. Our motives are mixed. One sure thing; as soon as you begin a "holy fast" you quickly learn what controls you. We often cover up what is inside us, hide it even from ourselves. But if pride or temper or jealousy or pettiness are inside, they quickly surface when you start to fast. Begin to fast and immediately you are tempted to call attention to your "deep spirituality" of fasting (like the Pharisees Jesus told about), and our pride erupts. Begin to fast, get hungry, and you get mean! Begin to fast, and our prevailing sins quickly rise up to expose themselves.

Jesus told us not to call attention to ourselves when we fast. The Pharisees did that, and the only reward they received were pious words of self-commendation they heard from their own self-praising lips.

Experiences Of "Holy Fasting"

Over the years, so many beautiful and wonderful things have transpired in the lives of those who have opted for self-denial during Lent, and have engaged in some kind of "holy fast."

As a pastor, I encouraged my congregation to a "holy fast." They could give up whatever they chose for the six weeks of Lent, and seek to know Christ himself in richer ways during the discipline. One little five-year-old girl, Annette, heard my sermon on fasting. Annette's favorite food was Pop-tarts, a fruit-filled goodie that she had learned to pop into the toaster for herself. As she left the church that Sunday morning, before Lent began the following Ash Wednesday, she looked up at me and said, "I'm going to give up Pop-tarts for Jesus for Lent and my mommy is going to give up potato chips. She loves them better than anything!" Her mother, Judy, gasped in surprise. She didn't even know the child was listening to the sermon. And it was true, potato chips were her favorite food! So, in the face of her daughter's commitment to give up Pop-tarts, Judy knew she had no choice; it would be six long weeks before she could taste another potato chip!

One man, in the same church, gave up smoking his pipe for six weeks, and never took it up again. One woman gave up crossword puzzles and used that hour a day for more Bible study and prayer. Another woman gave up her soap operas on television and used the time to pray. One gave up gossiping at the office and said she never felt so "clean" since she quit running through the daily garbage of other people's lives. And some gave up one food or another, some gave up certain meals — but it was a great joy, as their pastor, to see how the external actions began to penetrate their hearts, their spirits, and their lives. Changes began to take place in the church, in the families, and in the spirit of the congregation. A "holy fast" is a penetrating energy, and it gives new life and strength to all it touches where Christ is made the aim and center of it all.

My spouse and I find, personally, that Lent is the richest time of the entire church year for us. Our "holy fast" of six weeks may mean we fast on our "indispensable" coffee, on desserts and sweets, or maybe it is breakfast, or we fast on lunch. But the important truth is that the journey — the journey of repentance, of self-denial, the "holy fasting" — make the path to the cross inexpressibly sweet and unbelievably rewarding.

The fact is, whatever we "give up" is infinitesimally small when compared to the magnitude of the Savior's sacrifice on the cross-tree, but still it does in a tiny way let us experience some of his suffering, too.

An American businessman went to Oberammergau to see the famous Passion Play. He went backstage to meet Anton Lang, who then played the part of Christ. Noticing, in the corner, the great cross which Mr. Lang carried in the play, the tourist stooped to lift it to his shoulder, but he couldn't move it even one inch off the floor. It was made of heavy iron-oak beams. Amazed, the man turned to Lang and said, "I thought it would be light, hollow. Why do you carry a cross that is so terribly heavy?" Anton Lang replied softly, "Sir, if I did not feel the weight of the cross, I could not play his part."

True, you and I will never know the agonizing pain nor the tremendous load of the Christ-Cross, but a "holy fast" will keep us reminded of the direction we are headed and that his cost was far, far more than ours!

Lent 1
Deuteronomy 26:1-11

Are You A Basket Case?

We have a large, cylindrical basket by our fireplace which holds firewood. And we have another wonderful basket, perhaps a half-bushel in size, which was given to us by friends. It is hand-woven and crafted by a 92-year-old man who cut the tree, shaved off the strips, soaked them, and then created this lovely container; solid and stable, a treasure. I have a bread-basket; dainty, finely woven, and perfect — fashioned by a cultured, saintly woman in a church I served as pastor. Another everyday basket that now holds onions, potatoes, or whatever, came to us filled with fresh Georgia peaches. There are baskets all over the house; some given to us by children, others by friends. They came to us empty, or sometimes filled with jelly, homemade bread, or some other thoughtful gift. In nearly every room we have baskets which have silk or fresh flowers in them. A basket stands on the kitchen counter with fruit. Other small baskets in bathrooms hold candles, soap, or wash clothes. Each of these baskets evokes a remembrance of some person, event, or place.

I remember serving as pastor of a small, rural church which used handwoven baskets as offering plates. And baskets carry dishes of wonderful food for almost every church dinner you have ever attended.

But how many times do you see people fill baskets and bring them to the altar of the sanctuary in a basket? Interestingly enough, in this text for Lent 1, the vessels the Hebrews were to use to bring their first fruits and tithes to the place of worship was a basket. Every translation I checked uses the word "basket" — not a cloth bag, nor a jar, nor an earthen vessel, but a basket! And, as these Israelites brought their baskets to the altar, they recited the events in their lives which had brought them to this place.

But, this musty, ancient, almost stuffy Old Testament lesson can have little meaning for us unless we, too, join them in remembrance of our own journey. Lent is a time of remembrance and, as we begin this six-week trek, we start by filling our baskets with recollections of the blessings of God upon our lives.

We Recollect The Past

These people of long ago said (freely translated), "Our father, Jacob, was a wanderer. Like a gypsy he went from southern Canaan to Haran and back and then he migrated to Egypt. We grew into a mighty nation, but we became slaves. It was not an easy time. We suffered, we toiled, we were mistreated, and in our misery we cried out to the Lord."

Can you, like these Hebrews, remember what life was like before your deliverance; before Christ set you free? Some of you can't recall, for you've been blessed with being a Christian from a very tender age. Many persons are baptized as babies. I love to baptize babies, so that they never know the full extent of what it is to be owned by the devil. They may, in future years, be bothered, oppressed, and tempted by him, but never know enslavement to the enemy.

I was converted at the age of 15 years, but I still have vivid recollections of the nightmare of not being free. I was afraid nearly all the time. I was afraid of the second coming, lest Christ appear and I would not go with the saints he had come to claim. I hated to go to bed at night, scared that I might die and my soul be eternally lost. Even though I prayed, I had no certainty that my prayers were heard, for a guilty conscience made me doubt that God would hear.

Like Pharaoh, the devil is a hard task-master. Sometimes it is difficult to be a Christian, but it is infinitely more difficult to be enslaved by Satan. He takes our lives and controls them until we are no longer free to make good decisions. We try, but we have no power to resist temptation. We acknowledge the truth of the Scripture which says, "The way of the transgressor is hard."

We are asked to recall our past bondage, for we forget so easily. Two American Indians were visiting New York City for the first time and were stopped on the street by an admiring older woman. "Are you a real Indian?" she asked one of the native Americans. "Yes, I am," he replied. "How do you like our city?" she inquired. "Fine," he answered, "How do you like our country?" We often take our Christian privilege rather lightly, for we have forgotten how much we are in debt. We forget how far we have come, how dramatic our rescue has been, and what great cause we have for gratitude and rejoicing. The Psalmist sang, (40:2) "He brought me up also out of the horrible pit, out of the miry clay, and set my feet upon a rock, and established my goings."

God has lifted us out of sinking sand to solid rock, from shades of night to plains of light, and from terrible bondage to marvelous freedom. Someone said, jubilantly, "Out of the mire and into the choir!" Whether we sing in the choir or not, God has certainly put a song in our hearts, a praise to our God. May we never forget how black was our darkness before divine light shone upon us! In our success, in our security, in our salvation, let us not forget God.

In Pennsylvania, there is a small, mining town called Centralia. More than 20 years ago a fire broke out in one of the many tunnels and shafts that honeycomb the earth underneath the town. Local officials tried to extinguish the fire, and failed. Then state, and finally federal, mine officials tried to put it out. But nothing seems to do it, it still will not quit burning. Every now and then a puff of smoke will seep through the surface and no one can forget that the fire is still burning down there. That's just how active and persistent sin is in us. The devil never stops trying to get at us. We are not self-sufficient, we are not independent, we cannot make it on our own.

Again and again God reminded his people — and us — "Remember and do not forget how you provoked the Lord your God to wrath in the wilderness (Deuteronomy 9:7)."

Their days had been filled with evil. They did monumental wickedness against God; they were angry, they rebelled, they grumbled and complained, they worshiped other gods, they were disobedient and God said, "Remember, and do not forget." It is so easy to forget how bad we have been, how sinful, how wicked, how desperate our plight. How easy it is to be proud, how difficult to be truly humble. Though we would never say it aloud, sometimes we privately think God is pretty lucky to have us and that we did him the favor to let him convert us.

But if we truly remember what our past has been, then we can, as we bring our baskets of remembrance, be . . .

Reminded Of Present Mercy

God wants to do something for us! Isn't that wonderful news? The story goes that Arnold Palmer was asked by an oil sheik to come and lay out and supervise the building of a golf course in Kuwait. Palmer went, built a magnificent course, and was paid extremely well for it. As he prepared to leave and return home, the sheik came to him and asked him what he could give him as a gift. "Nothing," Palmer said, "you've already paid me a fortune and I don't need anything at all." But the sheik persisted, "Isn't there anything I could give you? Just tell me, anything at all?" Finally, Arnold said rather nonchalantly, "O well, give me a golf club," and he thought nothing more of the incident. He got on a plane, flew home, and was met at the airport by his secretary, whose opening question was, "Mr. Palmer, what in the world are you going to do with the Westshore Hills Country Club?" We simply have no idea of how much God wants to help us, bless us, and redeem us.

The Israelites said, as they brought their baskets to the altar, "God heard our cries and brought us out of Egypt. With his mighty hand and outstretched arm he performed wonderful signs and miracles for us: he turned water into blood, caused great darkness to descend on our enemies, plagued them with locusts, flies, frogs, and boils. For us, he divided the waters of the Red Sea, fed us quail and manna in the wilderness, gave us water in the desert, and brought us to this land."

Those ancient peoples had a mighty Moses to plead their cause before Pharaoh to lead them from bondage. But when Satan and our sins held us captive, who would deliver us? Jesus is our Moses, and he carried far more than a simple rod in his hand. Jesus carried a heavy cross on his back and was nailed to that tree, instead of ourselves. On that lonely gibbet he purchased our redemption. What glorious mercy is his! It seems that God is foolishly in love with us. He seems to have forgotten heaven and earth, his own happiness and pleasure, and has given his entire deity to deal lovingly with us. Christ dies, not because he is sinful, but because we are. He gave everything to comfort me, to help me, to identify with me.

Of course we are not worthy; never have been, never shall be. Ted Bundy, the convicted mass murderer, was executed in the electric chair in Florida in January of 1989. He had been tried and found guilty of the death of a 12-year-old girl, and had confessed to at least 22 more murders. Yet, just before he died at 7:06 on that Tuesday morning, he was allowed to speak with his mother on the phone. She said to him; this man of the heinous crimes: "You will always be my precious son." We, of course, feel that his crimes were utterly despicable, but somehow no matter what he had done, they could not kill the love in his mother's heart. We don't think our own sins were quite of that magnitude; but then we have no real idea of how offensive sin is to a holy God, or we would bow our heads in shame. But however multitudinous our sins, how heavy our guilt, it can't touch the love that God has for us. He continues to rescue us with a mighty hand and outstretched arm on Calvary's cross-tree.

The Future

Those Israelites recited their thanks before the altar, and said, "God has finally brought us here to Canaan, this land of milk and honey, and we rejoice in all the good things he has given."

Well, today we bring our baskets — our hearts — divinely woven by the hands of our Creator Father, and we begin Lent by remembering past sins and present mercies. We are overwhelmed by his forgiveness and love. We have not yet reached our heavenly Canaan, but we are on the way. An old gospel song says, "We're on the way to Canaan land, We're on the way, a pilgrim band; Divinely guided day by day, We're on the way, we're on the way!"

There is an old, old story about an Indian chief who wanted to test the strength of his four sons. He asked them to run, in a single effort, as far up the side of a mountain as each of them could reach by his own strength. On the appointed day, the boys left at daybreak. The first returned with a branch of spruce, indicating the height he had attained. The second brought back a twig of pine. The third brought an alpine shrub, from much higher up the mountain. But it was by the light of the moon that the fourth son finally made his way back. There he came; worn and exhausted, his feet were torn by the rocks. "What did you bring, and how high did you ascend?" the chief asked. "Sire," the boy replied, "where I went there was neither spruce nor pine to shelter me from the sun, nor flower to cheer my path, but only rocks and snow and barren land. My feet are torn, I am exhausted, and I have come late . . ." But then a wonderful light came into his eyes and he added, "And, father, I saw the sea!"

Today, we remember with sorrow, our sins. We recall with gratitude our mercy and we look to the future with God. But in the future we still can only see the vague outline of the form that hanged on Good Friday's cross. We can't really see him, it is only by faith that we know he is there.

But one day, when the future is not a dim, distant hope but rather a clear and present reality, they will ask us what we see, and we will say: "I have climbed and climbed, sometimes slipping back into my old ways. Often the path was rough and I stumbled and fell, other times it was smooth and pleasant, but as I have climbed, I have finally arrived here in heaven's land of milk and honey, and I see Jesus! It was worth it all. The trials were really nothing. I'd do it again and again. A glimpse of Christ has erased all the trials and the sight of him has satisfied every longing of my heart!

But not yet. This is only part of the journey now that we have run. We have not arrived, but we have glimpsed the future glorious, and we press on. Today our baskets hold only our poor hearts of love, but as ordinary as our gifts are, we offer them to him, and he accepts them and calls them, because of his fathomlessness for us, precious. Hallelujah! What a Savior!

Lent 2
Genesis 15:1-12, 17-18

The Problem With A Promise

You have all made promises; and kept them, but some you have broken. Maybe you didn't intend to break it, but when the time came to fulfill it, it simply wasn't in your power to keep it. Or, upon re-thinking it, you decided it wasn't a good promise, so you reneged upon it.

And, you've had promises made to you; and they've been kept — some of them, but who has not been hurt by having a promise made, and then broken?

What parents have not heard their child exclaim at some point, "But you promised me!" Obviously, some promises are easier to keep than others. A mother told of overhearing a conversation between her two daughters. The younger child had had considerable difficulty in trying to learn how to know which shoe went on which foot. The older girl said to her younger sister, "Listen, I'm going to tell you something and I want you to remember it the rest of your life. Do you promise to remember this the rest of your life? Promise for as long as you live?" The younger child meekly said, "Yes." The older one said, "Okay. Here it is. Whenever you put on your shoe, if it hurts, you've got it on the wrong foot!" Now that's an easy enough promise to keep, but have you heard any of these and had them broken? "I promise I won't tell a soul." "I promise to love, honor, and cherish." "I promise to be faithful." "I promise to pay the bill." "I promise to never do it again." "I promise to not forget." "I promise to be there on time." "I promise you this is the truth."

Promises! Promises! What good are they if all you have is someone's word? They may be able to perform, or they may never intend to keep it. They may not have the power to do it, it may slip their mind, and on and on it goes. That's the problem with a promise. Sometimes the word of another is simply not enough. We need a guarantee!

Look at the problem with a promise.

The Promise And The Promiser

We Christians are people of promise. It requires faith to believe in a promise that is not immediately kept, and that is the lesson of this text.

Abraham and Sarah began a pilgrimage of hope when they left Haran. About all that Abraham had was a promise (Genesis 12:1-4a), a promise that the God who called him would make of him a great nation, that God would bless him, that God would make his name great, and Abraham himself would be a blessing.

But you can't be made into a great nation without descendants and you can't have descendants without having children, and Sarah was barren, and all this childless couple have is a promise that looks impossible. Abraham is already 75 years old and Sarah is 65. And they have a promise that God will make of them a great nation. If they had told us about it we would have thought: "They must have misunderstood. God must not have been speaking literally. Surely this is a Scripture that must be de-mythologized; it must have a 'spiritual application.' After all, 65-year-old women do not bear children, so either Abraham must get himself another, younger woman to bear him a child (Abraham thought of that and tried it), or they must adopt. But one thing is sure, this particular promise must not be taken literally. After all, God expects you do use good, common sense!"

But God did promise an heir to Abraham and he meant it. But how can you trust in a promise when the evidence against its being kept is all around you? That's Abraham's dilemma — and the same problem is often ours.

Abraham is called the "father of faith," but it is not a title that was easily earned. Abraham's faith is not a peaceful, pious, wishy-washy faith. His faith and conviction in the promise of God is hard-fought and deeply-argued.

The text opens with God's promises being re-stated: "Fear not!" Abraham has probably come to terms with his barrenness; is learning to live with it. Nothing was ever going to change. Then God shatters that kind of thinking with his "Fear not!" and then God repeats the promise. Abraham retorts and protests and argues about the delayed promise (vv. 3, 4). He tells God what God already knows (we do that a lot, too): "I have no offspring, I am childless, a slave in my house will be my heir." Abraham feels a lot of anguish over this. He had no son and a "reasonable substitute will not do."

Then God re-asserts his promise, shows Abraham the stars, but really offers him nothing more, nothing new, nothing except his Word! After this discussion, all Abraham has, is still just a promise, just a Word. He has nothing in writing (AT&T dares you to ask their competitor to put their claims in writing), no proof, no guarantee. Now the test of faith really begins. Now Abraham must decide if God is God, if his Word is good, if — after all this time — in spite of the evidence to the contrary, if he can count on this promise. And Abraham believed! No wonder he is called the "father of faith!"

Abraham decides that God, not the circumstances, make the promise believable. He decided that the same God who makes stars can also make a son for an old, barren, childless couple. Abraham didn't decide to believe because he felt new life in his loins, nor because Sarah came and told him she was experiencing morning sickness, nor because a new fertility drug for older women had just been approved by the FDA. He simply believed he could rely on the promise of the Promise-Maker.

God has given us promises, too — thousands of them — in his Word. I haven't checked them all out, yet, but the ones I've tested and tried I have found to be unshakably certain. God promised: "Come to me, all ye who are weary and heavy laden, and I will give you rest." I came and he did. He said, "If we confess our sins he is faithful and just to forgive our sins and to cleanse us from unrighteousness." I did and he did. Jesus promised, "I will send the Holy Spirit upon you." He did. He said, "The Lord will give peace to his people." I have found that he does. The Word promises, "Delight yourself in the Lord and he will give you the desires of your heart." It's true, he does. He promised, "Seek ye first the kingdom of God and his righteousness, and all these things shall be added unto you." It's a fact. He assured us, "Lo, I am with you alway." He is."

I keep finding, or hearing, or reading a promise, and he keeps making it true. I have never known one of God's promises to fail.

These days of Lent remind us that God promised to send to the world a Messiah, a Redeemer, his Anointed One. And for six weeks we look again in wonder at that fulfilled "Word that became flesh and dwelt among us." We took that promise made incarnate as God became reality in that little baby boy born in Bethlehem's barn and we nailed him to a tree. Did Isaiah say more than he realized when he said, "He was pierced for our transgressions, he was crushed for our iniquities, the punishment that brought us peace was upon him, and by his wounds we are healed (Isaiah 53:5)." Can we ever again doubt any promise God has made when we see the promised Savior hanging before us in the throes of death as in agony he fulfills God's Word?

So, as people of faith, we make the assumption that because of who the promiser is — none other than God himself — that we can believe it. Abraham made the basic assumption that God was God, that his Word was enough, and that assumption became an unshakable assurance. Helmut Thielicke said, "Taking God seriously means taking him at his Word and giving him the chance to act the way he has said he will act."

A woman came up to an evangelist after hearing him preach, and said that she could not understand salvation. The preacher said, "Mrs. Franklin, how long have you been Mrs. Franklin?" "Why, ever since I was married," she replied. "And how did you become Mrs. Franklin?" he asked. "When the minister said, 'Wilt thou have this man to be thy wedded husband,' I just said 'Yes.' " "Didn't you say, 'I hope so,' or, 'I guess so,' or 'I'll try to'?" asked the minister. "No," she said, "I just said, "I will." Then the evangelist pointed to God's Word and said, "God is asking you if you will accept his Son. What will you say to that?" Her face lighted up and she said, "Why, how simple it is! Isn't it odd that I didn't say 'yes' a long time ago?" This is the simple faith in God's Word that is called for. God has promised that if we come in repentance and faith, that he will receive you for Christ's sake. Trust it, count on it, try it, believe it. Remember, you can never break God's promises by leaning upon them.

The Promise Delayed

The problem with a promise is always the delay, the waiting. We have lived with so many broken promises made by humans that we've come to expect the same from God. Some months ago I preached a revival. In the dining room of the motel where I stayed while I was there, was a sign. It read: "We promise friendly and courteous service at reasonable prices. If for any reason we fail to live up to this promise — please don't tell anyone!" But God lives up to his promises. He does not break them. But he does sometimes delay. To wait a very long time is a strong theme in this text. Abraham has no heir, and in spite of having a promise, he must wait still longer.

We are not accustomed to waiting. We don't like to wait on the phone, we resent being put on "hold," we'd rather not wait in a long line, we don't want to wait for a diet to show its effect, we don't like to wait our turn. We are a fast-food, fast-service, fast-car/plane/boat people and are impatient when we have to wait. We now have fast, drive-through viewing for the dead so we don't have to wait. "Well, I'm not going to wait any longer," is a phrase you hear nearly every day of your life. So, when we deal with the promises of God we are equally impatient and are prone to conclude if the answer is not given now, it never will be.

But a promise is a gift, a grace from God, and gifts cannot be forced nor hurried. Our futures stay in the hand of the God who gives them.

God's move toward Abraham was free and unconditional. Abraham needed only to trust, and he did. "He believed God, and God credited it to him as righteousness (v. 6)." It is only an unsure faith that wonders about delay. An unsure faith questions "When?" and "How?" A faith in the promise of the divine Promise-Maker believes and waits.

We cry, "O Lord, how long?" How long until I am well again, how long until my children are saved, how long until my marriage gets better, how long until you find me a job/husband/wife/house? And that's the test of our faith, just as it was for Abraham. We are like little children when we have to wait. A family was taking a trip by car, some distance away. Knowing the impatience of their young son, the parents cautioned him as they got into the car, "Now we will get there as soon as we can. We will get there. But don't keep asking when we are going to get there — understand?" After traveling some miles, from the back seat of the car the boy ventured this question, "Will I still be alive when we get there?"

We run by clocks and calendars, by schedules and timetables, so we assume God does, too. And we want him to tell us when, what time, what day, what year — forgetting that God does not limit himself to our puny plans and schedules. He has eternity and our days and minutes and years are not binding to him. Of course we argue and say, "But God, if you don't do it now, or by Tuesday, or next year, it will be too late." But that is putting human limitations upon God, saying, "He can't fix it," except in our time frame.

Abraham was 75 and Sarah was 65 when God gave them the promise — how easy it would have been for Abraham to say to God, "You'd better hurry — Sarah's not getting any younger. It's impossible now, but it's getting more so every day." Amazing, when you think about it, this "father of faith" had such simplicity of trust in the promise. Note the three words, "Abraham believed God." Don't you wish it could be written of us, "Barbara believed God." "John — Joe — Betty — your name — believed God." Habakkuk, the prophet, has some good words on this, "If it seems slow, wait for it; it will surely come, it will not delay (Habakkuk 2:3)."

The Promises Are Worth Waiting For

Let us never forget: the promises of God are worth waiting for! In a rather restrained fashion, our text suggests (vv. 17, 18) that somehow the mysterious and unseen presence of Yahweh is engaged in this action. Abraham has prepared a sacrifice of a heifer, a goat, a ram, a dove, and a pigeon to offer to God. It is then that the Lord comes to Abraham. He has a mysterious firepot with a blazing torch and the fire moves among the pieces of the sacrifice that Abraham has placed upon the altar. This is a curious, old, ritual act which suggests a solemn, weighty, binding of the two parties to each other. God is here making a covenant with Abraham, renewing again his promise of an heir and land.

This text makes us ask two large questions: Can Abraham trust? Can God be trusted? The answer in both cases is a resounding "Yes!" God put flesh on his word and gave Abraham a son. He had to wait for it — he was 75 years old when he first got the promise (Genesis 12) in Haran. Now, 25 years later, when he is a centenarian, the promise is fulfilled and Isaac is born.

God is always doing such things with his promises. God finally put flesh on his Word, and the promise was fulfilled, centuries later, when God gave the world Jesus. He always is true to his Word.

Lent's cross-bound journey is another reminder that the promised Redeemer came and lived and died that we might know God as Father; might have forgiveness of sins, and have life everlasting.

I haven't checked out all of the promises of God yet. But each one that I have ever relied upon has proven true and faithful. But there are still other promises God has made that are worth waiting for. I still claim them, though they haven't come to pass yet, but God's past record absolutely convinces me that he can be trusted for the future ones.

So, when Christ says, "I will come again," I believe it. No matter how long it is until it happens, I still believe in the second coming. He said, "I will go and prepare a place for you, that where I am, ye may be also." No matter when I die, I firmly believe I have a home in heaven waiting for me. He said, "Train up a child in the way it should go, and when it is old it will not depart from it." That promise has been partially fulfilled for me, but I believe it will happen. God will not let all the toil, teaching, prayers, tears, and love we give our children be wasted. I believe God.

The Problem Is Not In The Promise-Maker, But Receiver

We cannot just "decide" one day to have faith. It doesn't work that way. Abraham did not move from protest to confession and faith by persuading himself, or by talking himself into it. He simply accepted the disclosing Word of God. We, too, become practitioners of faith in all of our hopelessly, impossible situations by knowing the two things that Abraham came to know: God could be trusted, and he would trust God. That is why we can so lustily and confidently sing the lines of the familiar song, "Standing on the promises that cannot fail, When the howling storms of doubt and fear assail, By the living Word of God, I shall prevail; Standing on the promises of God!"

Lent 3
Exodus 3:1-15

A Fireside Chat

Radio and television have introduced the nation to the fireside chat: dignitaries who sit down before a fireplace, and there, in a more or less person-to-person manner, address the listeners. The intention, of course, is that each hearer will feel it is a personal message on an important mater. Franklin Delano Roosevelt had fireside chats, via radio, when he was president. Later, Jimmy Carter did the same thing, only by television. Even Billy Graham on his Christmas special has, from time-to-time, sat by the fire and talked to us. But the fireside chat of our text is not an easy, comfortable, warm conversation. It is a mighty confrontation of God with Moses that will forever change the destiny of the man and the Hebrew nation!

Moses, in the training school of God, has come a long way already. He was set afloat, by his mother, on a waterbed on the Nile. He was found by Pharaoh's daughter and subsequently grew up in the king's court. After his Egyptian education he was found interfering with a quarrel between two men, and wound up killing one of them. He ran away to Midian, married a wife, and is now living out his day-to-day existence herding sheep in the desert for his father-in-law.

As old as this encounter by the fire was, it still has lessons for us today:

Curious

In the midst of that drab, everyday, humdrum existence God invades his life with intentions to use him in his mighty plan to deliver his people. He has heard their groaning, seen their tears, remembered their covenant with Abraham, and is moved with concern and compassion for them. And when God is concerned, it's not an easy, little, temporary thought of "I'm-sure-sorry-and-I-wish-I-could-help," but it is an active empathy that enters into the problem with Divine help.

And Moses is the unlikely man that God intends to use for this purpose. Moses may not know it yet, but all of his life, until now, has been a preparatory school for God's larger plan for him. I wonder if we realize that each day, whether it is dreary or exciting, we are just getting ready for the next step in God's plan for us? We are people of destiny!

It is here, in the text, that Moses becomes curious because of a phenomenon. Do you know what a pheomenon is? I lately heard a definition: "If you go out to the country and see a large field with a cow in it, that is not a phenomenon. If, over that same field, you hear a lark singing, that is not a phenomenon. But, if, in that field, you see a cow, sitting on a thorn bush, singing like a lark, that is a phemonemon! But what Moses sees is no joke. It is actually a miracle. God grabs Moses' attention with a burning bush. Moses must have thought: "Odd, how did that bush catch fire out here in the desert?" But even more strange, as he continues to gaze at the bush he noted it was not burned up! Things that burn are ordinarily consumed by the flames, or they melt down, or are blackened, or turn to ashes. Why is this bush different? So, curious, he thought, "I'll go closer. I'll see why it does not burn up. I'll get the answer. I'll figure it out. I'll see why!"

How typical of us humans. Most of us figure that anything we don't fully understand, just give us time and we can figure it out. We can find the answer, we can solve it. After all, everything has a sane, sensible, logical, rational, cause-and-effect solution. "Give me time and I'll find it!" Of course, God created us to think, and human solutions are fine in most instances. But some things you can never explain by human logic. Miracles are not "explained" away. The only reason Moses ever found for a burning bush that was not consumed was God! Sometimes that's the only logical conclusion we can reach, too. It's God, plain and simple. No other conclusion will suffice.

No other answer makes sense. It's God, and that's all you can finally say! Of course, when you've said God, you've said it all!

Confident

Now begins the fireside chat. When God sees that he has captured, through his curiosity, the attention of his man, he calls his name, "Moses! Moses!" And Moses answers with what appears to be supreme self-confidence, "Here I am." This is the response of a man still in control of his own life. Moses has lived long enough to believe himself fairly capable. Things have always worked for him in the past. He's a self-made man; maybe not perfect, but others have done far worse than he. Of course, if we'd ask Moses (as we must also ask ourselves), he might have confessed that he maybe could have done better, but he is certainly not "all bad." Many of us would conclude the same: we are not perfect, but all-in-all, we've done fairly well as a wife, mother, father, husband, child, friend, worker, whatever — on a scale of one to ten, maybe we're not a ten, but we are at least a seven or eight, and what's so terrible about that? We have read books on self-esteem and patted ourselves on the backs until we believe most of our own press, and feeling pretty good about ourselves we look with magnanimity on others and say, "I'm okay and you're okay."

True, we further defend ourselves, maybe we are a bit self-centered, self-serving, self-concerned, self-confident; but what's wrong with that? If we don't watch out for ourselves, who will? Don't all the self-help books, programs, and courses say you have to have self-esteem, self-love, and self-worth before you can amount to anything? So, what's wrong with Moses' response, in the face of an unexplained miracle, to say with absolute self-confidence, "Here I am."

Of course there's nothing actually wrong with it. It's a fact that every human being must have a sense of value and worth in order to function well. It just seems sad that his self-confidence made him so secure that he was totally insensitive to the fact that he was standing on sacred soil. There was no hint that he ought to tread lightly here. He was rather rash, almost to the point of arrogance, as he stood on holy ground. Gregory Peck was standing in line, it is said, in a restaurant, waiting to be seated. Someone suggested, "Why don't you just tell them who you are?" Peck, with marvelous acumen replied, "When you have to tell them who you are, you aren't." Maybe we are too self-confident when we can't tell that the sacred has invaded our secular territory. Maybe our self-confidence has blinded us to our need to fall in awe and reverence before a holy God. Maybe, in the presence of the Divine, we are a tad too confident.

Confused

God immediately puts Moses in place by commanding, "Slow down, don't come any closer. You are standing in a place you have never stood before. Take off your sandals. You are on holy ground." As the fireside chat continues, God explains further, "I am the God of your fathers; of Abraham, Isaac, and Jacob." Suddenly this self-confident man hides his face; his self-certainty disintegrates in the presence of the holiness and greatness of God!

Then God really nails his man, Moses. He tells him he is sending him as a deliverer to lead his people out of Egypt. Moses' answer is no longer a confident, "Here I am," but his response is now re-arranged into a confused, "Who am I?" It always happens; the awareness of God's holy self awakens in us a sense of our own smallness and sinfulness. When God is near we see ourselves as we really are. Most of us, deep down, in spite of all our self-esteem, in spite of all our braggadocio, in spite of all our declarations of worth, are not always so sure. Psychologists say that even the most successful of us often suffer from what they have named the "Imposter Syndrome." We have a feeling we are really very ordinary and, in spite of money, power, success, we just got lucky and don't really deserve it after all. It is especially true that when a sense of God's presence is felt, we begin to recall the lies we've told, the sexual sins we've indulged in, the tests we've cheated on, the shady deals we've arranged, the people we've hurt, the selfishness we've shown — oh, my, the things we remember when God is near!

When God comes near we become cowards, all. I heard a story of some office workers who were discussing weekend sports activities. One man said, "I can't indulge in water skiing, mountain climbing, snorkeling, or scuba diving because of my back." "What's wrong with your back?" asked a coworker. He replied, "It's got a big, yellow streak!" Our yellow streak begins to show when we are confronted by God. We are not so sure who we are and what our worth is. We can readily sympathize with Moses who plaintively now queries, "Who am I?"

Now, actually, Moses was, in fact, the finest, fittest man for the job of deliverer. His realization that he is on holy ground and in Divine Presence brings out a healthy, new humility in him, thus the "Who am I?" Strange, isn't it, the more fit we are, the less high the opinion we hold of ourselves. God can always use brokenness. It takes broken soil to produce a crop, broken clouds to give rain, broken grain to give bread, broken bread to give strength, and broken men and women for God to reveal his greatness through them. Martin Luther said, "God cannot make something of us until we are nothing."

A story is told of the funeral of Charlemagne, one of the greatest early rulers of the earth. The mighty funeral procession came to the cathedral, only to find the gate was barred by the bishop. "Who comes?" shouted the bishop. The heralds answered, "Charlemagne, Lord and King of the Holy Roman Empire!" The bishop replied for God, "Him I know not! Who comes?" The heralds, a bit shaken, replied, "Charles, the Great, a good and honest man of the earth!" Again, answering for God, the bishop replied, "Him I know not! Who comes?" Now, completely crushed, the heralds give answer, "Charles, a lowly sinner, who begs the gift of Christ." Then God's representative replied, "Him I know. Enter! Receive Christ's gift of life."

So now, this humbled Moses; confused, uncertain and insecure, begins to make excuses. Who can blame him? When such an overwhelming task is given and one sees oneself as we truly are, we all begin to make excuses. Moses asks, "Suppose I go to the Israelites, suppose I tell them my father's God sent me, suppose they ask me your name, what shall I tell them?"

Committed

God tells his man his name: "I AM THAT I AM." "You can fully commit yourself to me, Moses. I have committed myself to you in giving you my name. You can be, not self-confident, but God-confident!" In revealing his name, God is indicating that he has his being of himself . . . "I AM." God is self-existent, and dependent upon no other. He is both self-sufficient and all-sufficient. This is God's name forever; "I AM WHO I AM." He is eternal and unchangeable. God is himself the inexhaustible fountain of all being and bliss.

It is utterly mind-shattering to know that our Lenten journey is leading us to see our crucified Lord, the One who is exactly like God — nay, is God — the One who showed himself to Moses. The record says of Christ, "Jesus Christ, the same yesterday, today, and forever (Hebrews 13:8)." Jesus is making the same claim as God. The Son of God, who proceeded from the Father, calls himself by the same name; "Before Abraham was, I AM." Can it be, oh, yes, it can be, that Jesus is adopting the very same name that God revealed to Moses, is presenting himself to us a Yahweh-Jesus! All that God promised to be to Moses and his people is fully realized for us in Christ, our New Testament "I AM THAT I AM." What the Old Testament Lord was to the Israelites, so Christ, our New Testament Lord is to us. That means that all God is and was, so is Jesus to us. When he says, "I AM" it means he is for us, too, Deliverer, Provider, Guide, Protector. He has identified himself to us further by saying, "I AM the Bread," "I AM the Vine," "I AM the Good Shepherd," "I AM the Light," "I AM the Door," "I AM the Way, the Truth, and the life," "I AM the Resurrection and the Life," "I AM the Redeemer," "I AM the Savior." When God tells you his name, it means that all of the advantages inherent in its meaning become yours and mine. All that God in Christ was, he is, and will be forever and ever!

The "I AM" Is With Us

A man once decided to buy a puppy for his little girl. He took her to the pet store and there, among all the many choices she might have made, she finally picked a scrawny little puppy for her own. Her daddy asked, "Are you sure you want this one?" "Oh, yes," she responded, "I love them all, but this one loves me. Can I name him, too?" When the father said she could choose what the new pet would be called, the child held it close to her face and said, "I'm going to call him 'Mine.' "

The fireside chat between Moses and God is ended for now. Moses leaves the spot called "Holy Ground" and goes to unhallowed places to become the Deliverer God called him to be. But the great I AM who promised to be with him, goes along. For the great I AM is not only beside burning bushes, but in conflict with the enemy, providing manna and water in the wilderness, on long marches with grumbling people, and finally leads them to the Promised Land. And our great I AM is not only with us as we worship in the holy places we've named as church, but he is with us on the dusty road of life, he is dying for us on a cross, he is interceding for us as Intercessor, he is Guide, and Comforter, Savior, and Friend, and finally will lead us to heaven's promised land. Our "I AM" is always in the here and the now!

Lent 4
Joshua 5:9-12

Healing For The Past

Occasionally I hear a senior citizen complain, "I just can't remember names like I used to," or, "I can't remember a thing anymore." Reminds me of a *Peanuts* cartoon strip I saw some time ago. Charlie Brown says, "My grandfather loves to sing hymns. He can remember the words to over a hundred hymns." Linus asks, "Does he sing in the choir?" Charlie replies, "No, he can't remember where the church is!"

But the problem for many is not that they can't remember, but they can't forget. Psychologists remind us that the past plays a powerful part in how we live our lives in the present. They estimate that we spend as much as 50 percent of our emotional energy trying to repress painful memories. Some of us have had experiences that have traumatized us in some way — and if they have not been softened for us — we still feel the effects in nearly every area of our lives. Maybe some have been abused emotionally or physically as children, or maybe you lived in poverty, or ignorance, or with parents who fought all the time. Maybe you came from a broken home, or were raped, or someone died; all sorts of things that run the gamut of human experience may have occurred in our past, and we carry the baggage of all of it with us still. We can't fully live today because half of our power is being used to deal with something that happened in the past.

Let us look at God's way of dealing with our past . . .

The Past Erased

These almost obscure verses in Joshua give us some clues as to how our past can be healed with the help of God.

The Hebrews have crossed the Jordan, and finally, 40 years after leaving the bondage of Egypt, they have reached the borders of the Promised Land. Gilgal is their first stop as they begin to establish a beachhead in Canaan. In front of them is Jericho and a hundred other places to be conquered before the land is fully theirs. Gilgal became holy ground to the people of Israel. It was the base of their operations against the enemy. They would return here again and again. Gilgal means "roll." The text says, "the reproach has been rolled away."

It is at Gilgal that the rite of circumcision is put into practice again. For the 40 years of the wilderness wandering, it had not been practiced. Circumcision was the seal of God's covenant with Abraham (Genesis 17:10-14). It was the mark of the promise that Abraham and his seed would possess Canaan. But it was suspended for 40 years because the people had been unbelieving and disobedient.

So, after crossing Jordan, and setting up the 12 stones to mark the great event of arrival, the first thing to take place at Gilgal was to have all the males submit to this painful and humbling rite of circumcision. The New Testament speaks of "the circumcision which is not made with hands." Paul said, "And ye are complete in him, which is the head of all principality and power: in whom also ye are circumcised with the circumcision made without hands, in putting off the body of the sins of the flesh by the circumcision of Christ (Colossians 2:10, 11)."

When the Israelites became obedient — and were circumcised — the text says, "The reproach of Egypt has been rolled away from you." The past is erased and eradicated, the shame of it is rolled away. Don't you wish that could happen to you? Would it not be a wondrous healing if the past with all its pain and hurt and guilt could be taken away?

Perhaps you have a past that still causes you pain, memories that make you blush with shame, your closest friend doesn't know about it, your conscience often stabs you, your guilt consumes you, you dare not think of it at night or you'll never sleep a wink, sometimes you think it will drive you crazy — oh, how the memories of the past burn!

In the play, *Richard the Third*, Shakespeare's character, King Richard, walks the stage and confesses, "My conscience has a thousand several tongues, and every tongue brings in a several tale, and every tale condemns me for a villain."

I doubt seriously that there is a single person reading this message, or hearing it preached, who has not had memories in their past that plague them almost beyond endurance!

I read of a young woman who got drunk at a party and passed out. She didn't remember anything after that, except that some weeks later she discovered that she was pregnant. Hoping to avoid embarrassment, she had a quick abortion. Now she keeps having nightmares in which a baby chases her. He is crying out to be born. The dreams have gone on for months, and she is now an emotional cripple. The past is killing her.

A fairly recent novel, *Any Day Now,* by Elizabeth Quinn, tells of a Vietnam veteran who is eaten alive with guilt because he scrambled aboard a chopper when it came to lift the wounded to safety, but it meant leaving his buddy, Leon, behind, bleeding on the battlefield. Nick can no longer live with the guilt, so he spends time, money, and effort to locate Leon, even if it means his own cowardice will be exposed.

I asked an army officer who had had to make many judgments on the field of battle, how he felt about them in retrospect, and this fine, tender-hearted man said to me, "There are a few decisions I've made that still haunt me." Our memories can burn.

A paper reports the account of a woman whose baby was sleeping in a crib and she was showing a new dress to her friend. She draped a plastic dry-cleaner bag over the crib-rail for a moment. Her friend said, "You'd better take that plastic bag away before you forget it." But she didn't. She left the room and a breeze from the window lifted the bag off the rail and onto the infant's face. She came in later to find him dead. Now, six years later, every time she hears a child cry, or passes a dry-cleaners, she is devastated by her memories of the past. Where is healing for that kind of torture and self-blame?

How were these Israelites to be healed of the sharp pain in their past: the past that reminded them that they had lived as slaves? They had had no homeland. They had no independence. They made bricks without straw and bowed to every whim of a despotic ruler who treated his animals better than they. And how could they forget their own grumblings against the God who was helping them, their disobedience, their lack of faith, their idolatry, their shame? What do you do with a past like that?

What do we do with our past? Our memories eat us alive. The things we've done, the things we've left undone, the things done to us — they all sneak up on us and kill us. How can we forget: the way I treated my parents, my husband, my wife, my children, my friends — or how they treated me. The money I stole, the lies I told — or the money stolen from me and the lies told about me. My sexual sins, my failures, my foolishness, my mistakes, my bad choices — worst of all my sins. With Luther we cry, "Oh, my sins! My sins!" Our memories are so ravaging. We affirm the words of the Psalmist who cried out, "My sins are ever before me (Psalm 51:3)."

Then the Scripture says, for these Hebrews, when obedience begins again and faith returns, "God rolls the reproach away." Imagine that! We can give Christ our painful past and our terrible memories and let him forgive and heal them all! Imagine no longer carrying the load of the past with you! You can forget it — it's forgiven! The past is covered by the blood. The sins are gone, cast into the deepest sea. "The reproach is rolled away!"

And now . . .

The Present Can Be Enjoyed

The nation is now in a new land, and there is new life for them there. The past is rolled away and the present can be enjoyed. Just four days after crossing the Jordan they observe the Passover.

The Passover had been observed only twice before; once when they went out of Egypt, and the other time was at Mount Sinai. Since then, no Passover: this feast of worship, remembrance, and fellowship had been abandoned altogether — not by their choice, but by God's command. God had commanded that no uncircumcised person partake of the Passover (Exodus 12:48). You see, they had forfeited their right to it by living in unbelief and disobedience. Because of that, no Passover. There can never be any real, true, worship of God if there is disobedience to God in our lives.

But as soon as the rite of circumcision was renewed, they kept the Passover. The original Passover marked the beginning of Israel's national life and inaugurated the day when God redeemed them from the long and oppressive Egyptian bondage.

The New Testament clearly identifies the death of Christ as the fulfillment of the Passover. John the Baptist hailed Jesus as "the Lamb of God who takes away the sin of the world (John 1:29, 36)." According to John's chronology, Jesus was hanging on the cross at the precise time when the Passover lambs were being slain. Paul categorically declares, "Christ, our Passover Lamb, has been sacrificed (1 Corinthians 5:7, 8)."

So, the fulfillment of the Passover, we Christians believe, is in the sacrifice of Christ who "himself bore our sins in his own body on the tree." He, God's Lamb, was substituted in our place. He bore sin's penalty in our stead, and we go free! Christ died for us, Christ died instead of us!

The foundation of Israel's rejoicing was their costly deliverance from Egypt. The foundation of the Christians' rejoicing is in our far, far costlier deliverance from sin. Christ, our Paschal Lamb, has been slain, and because of the shedding of his precious life-blood, we have been set free!

That's the very reason we can be delivered from the pain of our past — why our memories can be healed. It is not possible for us to just decide to "forget it all;" something has to neutralize the pain and Christ alone can do that. "But," some would say, "I've had horrible things happen to me!",

"I've done some terrible, heinous deeds." "Can they be forgiven?" Indeed, they can be forgiven, and what is more, our slain Lamb not only, with his cleansing healing, covering blood forgives, but he also forgets!

The story is told of a little Filipino girl who claimed she actually talked to Jesus. The people of her village got all excited about it, and the word even spread to other villages, finally reaching even the Cardinal's palace in Manila and a monsignor was appointed to investigate the phenomenon, to see if the claims of the child were valid. The girl was summoned to the palace for a series of interviews. At the end of the third inverview the monsignor felt ready to throw up his hands. In frustration he exclaimed, "I don't know whether you're for real or not. But there is one acid test. This next week, when you talk to Jesus, I want you to ask Jesus what I confessed at my last confession." The little girl agreed. So when she came back the next week, the monsignor immediately asked, "Well, my dear girl, did you talk to Jesus this past week?" "Yes, your Holiness," the little girl replied. "And when you talked to him, did you remember to ask Jesus what I confessed at my last confession?" "Yes, your Holiness, I did," she said. "Well," the monsignor eagerly said, "when you asked Jesus what I confessed, what did he say?" The little girl immediately replied, "Jesus said, 'I've forgotten!' " That's what Jesus does! And what wondrous freedom there is in that knowledge. To be so freely loved and so freely forgiven that it is forgotten. I believe it, for even human love will do it sometimes, if love is strong enough. My husband and I have been married for 17 years, and his love for me is such that he often seems to forget any mistakes I've made. He'll tell you what a great cook I am, completely forgetting the times a meal has been below par. He'll trust me with driving his new car, never seeming to remember that once I drove his car with less than 300 miles on it, and another driver took the fender off of it! He'll tell you how good, and sweet, and thoughtful I am, conveniently forgetting those other times when I'm not. So, God, in love far greater than we can know, when we repent of our sins, forgives and forgets. Awash then, in that kind of love, we finally realize that we can also forgive ourselves and others, and healing for the past comes to us through our crucified Passover Lamb!

It is said that Franz Schubert once wrote in the margins of one of his symphonies some directions to the conductor. In one place he wrote, "As loud as possible!" Then a little later he directed, "Still louder!" How can you be still louder when you've already been as loud as possible? Something like that is true when we realize what God has done for us in Christ. We come to his cross with our past and our sins, and his blood covers all of them — neutralizes them in the crimson flood. That is as wonderful as anything we can ever imagine! And yet is more than wonderful when we realize we are not only forgiven, but the past is cast into the sea of his forgetfulness, never to be remembered against us anymore. Our Passover Lamb, hanging on Good Friday's Cross, is the Divine healer for all that has gone before in our lives!

This means, then, that . . .

The Prospect Is Excellent

These Hebrews have become once more an obedient people. They can enjoy, through the Passover, the holy fellowship again. That doesn't mean it's all over with, that there is no more work to do, no more battles to fight. The end is not yet, but the prospect is excellent. They are now working with God, not against him. A three-year-old boy named Michael listened attentively to a Sunday morning sermon. Afterward, his father asked him what he had learned, and the child commented, "Jesus died so that we could have ever-laughing life." That's almost true, you know. The path of the just is as a shining light that shines brighter and brighter as we walk with the Lord.

Notice that there are three successive days mentioned in this portion of the text: on the 14th day they kept the Passover, the very next day they ate of the corn of the land, and on the day after that the manna ceased. How quickly God responds to us when we become obedient!

The manna was wilderness food; it suited a wilderness journey. God supplied their food in the desert until corn was available. God always takes care of his children's needs. But you don't always need a radical miracle — as the manna was — when you get to a productive land. The exceptional and the extraordinary are means that God uses for us, but the normal, ordinary methods are how he usually supplies. You don't need to become, as Christians, dependent upon emotional thrills, spiritual excitement, and spectacular experiences. The "corn of the land" may seem mundane, but it is nourishing and good. God, in the everyday business of life is with us for guidance and strength, and for fighting evil in this world.

For the Israelites, the wilderness journey is over, the food that suited it is finished, and the new life is beckoning them with the promise of God's further blessings. For us, the past is forgiven, forgotten, and blotted out by the shed blood of our Lord. Now we live each day unto him in the new land. There may be battles ahead for us, as there were for the Hebrews, but God has promised to be with us all the way and we will ultimately triumph.

The late Frank Bateman Stranger, former president of Asbury Seminary, died in 1986. Those who knew him knew he had devoted his life to making disciples for Christ. He had great integrity and a tremendous faith. Someone told us of his death. In his final days he had a hospice nurse with him. One day, not long before he died, wanting to know just how aware he was, the nurse asked him if he knew what year it was. He said, "73." He did not know the year. She said, "Do you know who I am?" He smiled, but shook his head in confusion. He did not know who she was. Then the nurse asked, "Do you know where you are?" And Dr. Stanger firmly responded, "Chapter Eight — Romans Chapter Eight!" He knew where he was! "For I am convinced that there is nothing in death or life, in the realm of spirits or superhuman powers, in the world as it is or in the world as it shall be; neither the forces of the universe, nor the heights nor the depths, nothing in all creation that can separate us from the love of God which is in Christ Jesus." That's right, nothing can separate us from him!

There is full, total, and complete healing for the memories that burn, for the pain-producing past, and it's all in the prospect of the Christian who has come to know Jesus Christ, our Passover Lamb, as Savior and Lord!

Lent 5
Isaiah 43:16-21, 25

A "New And Improved" Jesus?

Next to "love," the word "new" is one of the most overworked words in our world. If it isn't new, we immediately consign it to ancient history. A minister friend, tells of speaking to a group of seventh grade confirmands. They were at a rather rustic retreat center. One boy came up to him, saying, "Boy! Is this place old! In the bathroom you have to turn on two faucets to get hot and cold water!" New and old is always relative, of course, but we quickly tire of the old and readily embrace the new as better.

This text is the announcement of God that he is doing a "new thing (v. 19)." Actually there are several new things mentioned in this account. God is dealing with exodus; three of them, in fact. The first exodus was from slavery in Egypt, the second exodus was from slavery in Babylon, and the third exodus (v. 25) was a spiritual exodus; slavery from sin.

We Like The New And Try To Improve On The Old

We live in a throw-away society, and usually we buy something that is new to replace the old, rather than trying to repair it. We've found it is generally cheaper to buy a new coffeemaker, a new toaster, a new iron, a new razor, a new hair dryer, or whatever, than to have it repaired. Besides, new is shinier, is maybe more trouble-free, is more popular, smells good, feels good, tastes good and is usually more attractive. We love new homes, new cards, new jobs, new styles, new foods, new clothes, new cosmetics, new diets, new lovers — if it's new, it gets our attention.

And if a product is one that we've been using, and we are contented with it, we are all the happier if we see it advertised as "new and improved." So we get rid of the old toothpaste, nail polish, cosmetics, detergent, computer, anything else you want to name, and buy the "new and improved" because it is supposed to be bigger, better, superior, and "good for you." Of course, many "new and improved" items really are far superior to the old, so who would want to stay with a passe product?

Who, for instance, wants to go back to the telephone of 50 years ago when today's telephone is obviously new and improved, with better service, easier and faster and clearer communication, and a multitude of services unheard of only a decade ago? Who wants to go back to the one-color black Ford of some years ago when you now have a wide-open market of far superior automobiles today? Who would really want to regress to the "good-old-days" that actually were not all that good if you had to live in them now?

I remember that when I was a small child my mother put the ice-card in the window of our house, indicating how much ice for the ice man to leave for the ice box in our kitchen. On most days the side indicating 25 pounds would be turned to say we would take that much that day. On a Saturday, providing mother had enough money, she would turn the card upside-down, showing a 50 pounds sign, so that we'd have enough ice to last until Monday. And on a really special day, when the children were all home, she might turn the card over and indicate we wanted a 100-pound chunk of ice! Wow! I always thought how impressed the neighbors must be as they saw how much ice we were ordering that day! That meant that 50 pounds would be placed in the ice box and the other 50 pounds would be wrapped in newsprint and placed in a big galvanized wash tub and covered with an old quilt, and sometime that afternoon we would make home-made ice cream! We small children would run out to the ice truck when it arrived, and watch the man as he took his ice pick and chipped off the size block we had ordered. Occasionally a sliver would fly free on the bed of his truck and we'd grab it and suck on it until it disappeared. They don't make ice today in any shape that tastes as sweet and cool and refreshing as that ice did! But all in all, while it served its purpose, the food was never really chilled, and the ice pan under the ice box, would run over from the melting ice and make a path across the kitchen linoleum that had to be mopped up. It was really pretty messy, but the best we could do. The chances are good, however, if you ever had an ice box, that this story has awakened all kinds of memories of your own and we could all become pretty sentimental and nostalgic just thinking about the past. But for me, that's all it is: good memories and nice sentiment, but I don't want to go back to the old ice box of my childhood. I like having a cold refrigerator with a freezer on the side, with an ice-maker that spills out cubes by just pressing a shiny piece of chrome on the door. I never want to return to the old oak box with a pan that runs over on the floor, just because you forgot to empty it.

All of this is to say, if it's "new and improved" and works better, and faster, and is easier, and nicer — fine! Why go back to the lesser when the better is at hand? But . . .

Some Old Things Are Better Left Unchanged

God, too, is always doing something that is newer and better. He is continually surprising us with a fresh idea, with doing a new thing. God made a glorious deliverance for his people at the first exodus when he delivered them from the terrible slavery in Egypt. They talked about it for years, and remembered the event annually at each Passover. Then, 910 years later, he did another new thing. This is the event promised in this text. God is delivering his people from slavery and bondage in Babylon. But still he is not finished yet: He has an even better plan for his people. Some 1,960 years later, God ushers in the third exodus and delivers his people from the slavery of sin by sending a Savior into the world.

But, since then, some 1,994 years later, no other "new thing" has been offered by God. Why not? Could it be that

God has no better plan, no greater plan? Could it be that in sending Jesus he sent his best and you can't get better than the best? For nearly 2,000 years now we have been recalling the coming of Christ into our world. How long has it been since you got excited about this same old Jesus that appeared on the scene a couple of millenia ago? Why doesn't God "freshen" our experience? When the pastor talks about new life in Christ, the best most people can manage is a yawn. When we ask ourselves if we really are new creatures, we suspect we are the same old persons we've always been. The story of Jesus is an old, old story, it's time-worn and we wonder if there is not a "new and improved" Jesus somewhere that we can follow.

Of course there have always been those who try to sell us on a new way, a new truth, a new Lord, a new religion. Buddhism, Hinduism, yoga, transcendental meditation, mysticism, psychology, new age — the list goes on and on and on. There always have been, and always will be, those false teachers and teachings which purport to have something that is "new and improved" — better than Jesus.

The Mormons would tell you that Jesus Christ is not to be worshiped, and that his death on the cross was only partially effective in saving the sinner. Sun Yung Moon would claim that Jesus was a failure and that he, Moon, is the new Messiah. New age would have you believe that they have really good news, "God is within you; inside you and outside you — or wherever you want him to be." Unitarians would boast that their chief concern is to save bodies, not souls, as Jesus taught.

The fact is, there are today those who would push Jesus into antiquity as being outmoded, outdated, and unnecessary; and would attack those who cling to him and his "old truths." They would accuse Christians who hold to the biblical truth that you can only come to God for deliverance from sin's slavery through Christ, as being "intolerant of other religions," or of being "religious bigots," or of "putting God in a box," or of being "exclusivist." Friends, we must cling to the biblical doctrine that teaches the uniqueness of Jesus. It matters not if we are labeled as old-fashioned or antiquated: be that as it may, we must reject the relativism that regards all religions and spiritualities as equally valid approaches to God!

Someone is also trying to "improve" on what God's Word teaches. Isn't it interesting how that in every decade or so we get a new idea of what will fix all our religious problems, our membership decline, and our general apathy? So we meet in conclaves, conferences, consultations, and committees: we talk and discuss and brainstorm and finally hand down new recommendations that "just might work." After hours and hours and hours of consultation and conversation over secondary issues, we argue as to whether the church should be inclusive enough to welcome ministers who are homosexuals, whether marriage should be allowed for persons of the same sex, the pros and cons of the quota system, whether the hymns might be better if we would change the words, how important it is to sing or chant or speak the psalms, should we excise language that is sexist from the litany. But it is all just so much "blowing in the wind," for when all is said and done, we admit in defeat that our new ideas have not worked wonders after all, we come back to the basic conclusion that it is the same sweet, old, old story of "this same Jesus" that still speaks to the hearts of people in our time. It is Christ who delivers from sin's bondage, it is Christ who makes us new, it is Christ who puts a song in the heart, and it is Christ who offers hope to every hopeless man and woman of the human race. It is the teachings of Jesus that we should hold up to ourselves to see if our conduct and behavior measure up to him.

And even more important than his teachings, is this Jesus himself. Jesus is God himself in the world! This wondrous new event that God had in mind some 2,000 years ago began with the Incarnation. Jesus, the Incarnate God, was born of a virgin, nursed as a baby, grew and lived among us, died on the cross for our sins, and conquered death in his glorious resurrection!

Some people want Jesus plus something else — but Jesus plus anything else is heresy! There is only one gospel because there is only one Christ, and Christ, because of his death and resurrection, is himself alone the way to salvation.

Nor do we need a new Bible, nor a new set of principles, nor a new doctrine of Christian faith. We just need to obey the old. We don't need a new set of beatitudes, or new parables, or a new Lord's Prayer, or a new ten commandments. The manger isn't new and the cross isn't new. Jesus is not "new and improved." He is the same wonderful Lord who went to Calvary's cross-tree, died there, and promises to make us new! After all, you would not even consider thinking you need a new *Pieta* by Michaelangelo, or a new "Jesu, Joy of Man's Desiring," or a new "Hymn to Joy" by Beethoven would you? Could we ever be presumptuous enough to believe we could improve on God's sunsets, or his sunrises, or his roses, or his springtime? What audacity would presume to believe we could improve on his Jesus? No, you can't improve upon perfection. We don't need a new Jesus, we just need to repent of our same old sins, confess our faith in the Savior, and obey him every day of our lives!

This Same Old Jesus Wants To Make A "New And Improved You"

It is absolutely true that we can't improve upon Jesus. We measure ourselves by him, not him by ourselves. The question is not whether or not we are happy with Jesus, but is he happy with us? It's not that Jesus is like God, it is that God is like Jesus, and in knowing Jesus we know all that we need to know about God the Father.

Amazing as it seems, when we know Jesus we know what we need to know about ourselves as well. Today's culture encourages us to "know yourself," "love yourself," "understand yourself," "accept yourself." But when we realize that God intended us to be like Jesus, to be conformed to his image, is dreadfully marred and defaced in us. It is in Jesus that we see ourselves as we ought to be. It is only in Jesus that our sins can be forgiven. It is only in Jesus that we can be made new creatures. It is only in Jesus that we have any hope at all.

The horrible truth is that most of us bear very little similarity to Christ, our great Example. A *Peanuts* cartoon, some years ago, showed Lucy saying to Charlie Brown, "I hate everything! I hate everybody! I hate the whole world!" Charlie Brown responds, "But I thought you had inner peace." "I do have inner peace," retorted Lucy, "but I still have outer obnoxiousness!" So do most of us still find ourselves sort of obnoxious at times. We loudly sing the old gospel song, "What a wonderful change in my life has been wrought, Since Jesus came into my heart." But where is the change? Why are we so little different from what we've always been? Honestly, now, do you feel that you are very much different since you've become a Christian than what you were before? Martin Marty, one of the liveliest commentators on the American religious scene, reported in an article, "If just the Christians in America would quit their sinning, it would drastically reduce the crime rate in America." It did not look good for us Christians when the newspapers and television reported that someone called "Robin Hud" by the press, who claimed to be a born-again Christian, was accused of embezzling nearly $5 million from the U.S. government. Something is wrong when thefts take place in the church. I have had two billfolds stolen in my life, both of them had been left in a pastor's study and were taken while we were in the worship services. We really need to offer to Christ a "new and improved" me and you!

We have a copying machine in our home, and we wonder sometimes how we ever managed to get along without it in the past. But, I rarely use it without thinking of the story I heard about a couple of men who worked in the army in military intelligence. This work often required long, typed reports. One day, the soldiers were dismayed to find only one sheet of typing paper on the base, and it was a weekend. In desperation, they went to the base reproduction and printing facility and asked the soldier on duty there for some of the paper used in the copying machine. He told them it was against regulations to give out any copy paper; regulations stated that all he could do for them was to make copies. So, not wanting to argue with army logic, the men simply got the soldier to run off 300 copies of their one blank sheet of typing paper! Wouldn't it be nice if the image of Christ could so easily be stamped upon us? Instead, we find his image blurred and often unrecognizable in our lives.

Through faith in Christ, we have actually been made new creatures. Why then, do we all know of Christians who lie, steal, cheat, gossip, commit adultery, and seem to still walk in darkness? There is no doubt that salvation comes to us through the work of Christ, and Christ alone. But many of us have been justified by grace through faith, but have never been sanctified. Sanctification is the work of the Holy Spirit that prompts and empowers and produces good works in us.

You've heard it said of someone, "He's not the man he used to be," and that is often literally true. The American Medical Association released some figures which say that every minute, five million cells in the human body are destroyed and replaced. Eventually, we become a new person. This physical renewal takes place unconsciously, without our awareness or consent, but spiritual renewal demands our consent and awareness. That is where the work and help of the Holy Spirit comes in. As we affirm the Lordship of Christ, in total commitment, we must surrender our personal lives completely to Jesus. The privilege and responsibility of all Christians is to so live that the Presence of Christ radiates from our lives so that everyone who knows us will see Jesus and be drawn to the Savior.

The Scotch comedian, Harry Lauder, said that when he was a boy he used to be fascinated by a lamplighter who moved down the shadowed streets of the town. He could always tell where the man was, by the trail of light he left behind him. As we walk through life, do we leave a trail of light or darkness?

Christ would like to so possess us, and cleanse us, and remake us, that everyone who sees us would say we are "new and improved."

Passion/Palm Sunday
Isaiah 50:4-9a

Not "If" — But "How"?

There is no use in worrying needlessly. Some things you absolutely cannot change. And some things are too ridiculous for us to be concerned about. A *Peanuts* column shows Charlie Brown saying, "I couldn't sleep last night. I kept worrying about school, and about life, and about everything." Snoopy, the dog, walks away thinking, "I didn't sleep well either. All night long I kept worrying that the moon was going to fall on my head."

Some issues are already settled, and there is no point in useless anxiety, for we do not always have choices and options. For instance, it is not "if" you will have a master in this life, you will have one, but "who" will it be? It is not "if" you will die, for unless the Lord returns during your lifetime, you will die, but your option is "where" you will spend eternity. And it is not "if" you will know suffering in this world, you will, but your choice is "how" will you react to it?

The verses of this text are from the servant songs that played such a pivotal role in the early church's understanding of who Jesus was. Here we see Israel, collectively, called the servant of the Lord. Then the transition is made to a personal servant, whose office is "to bring Jacob to him." And then all of this is finally fulfilled in history in the person of Jesus, the Suffering Servant with the capital "S." Even in the face of suffering, physical abuse, and degradation, the servant does not shrink from his calling. He knows that God will not abandon him in his suffering, so he is obedient to his calling to serve God's people. Unless we would go to the 53rd chapter of Isaiah, we likely cannot find a better picture of Christ the Suffering Servant whom we know as Jesus.

This is Palm/Passion Sunday in the church year, and since passion means suffering, what better time to examine his suffering and ours; his reaction and our own? We, the servants of Jesus, follow in his train. We are not better than our Lord and he knew terrible suffering. John (13:16) reminds us; ". . . no slave is greater than his Master, and no messenger is greater than the one who sent him." And John warned us again (15:20), "Remember what I told you: 'No slave is greater than his Master. If they persecuted me, they will persecute you too.' " Jesus endured all kinds of physical suffering when he lived among us, even to his death on a cross. Along with the agonizing physical torment, there was also the shame, disgrace, humiliation, rejection, loneliness, abandonment, the broken heart. So, how can we even begin to think we will completely avoid suffering? As sure as we live and try to emulate Christ as our Master, we, too, will know pain. There is no escape. It is not a matter of "if" we will suffer, but "how" we will react to it.

But let us not despair. This does not mean that life will be all grief, and hurt, and pain, and sorrow. There are six times more mention of the word "joy" than the word "sorrow" in the Bible. "Glad" is used 10 times more than the word "sad."

As we look at the Suffering Servant, we get some good lessons as to "how" we face our pain.

Christ Learned From His Suffering — And So Can We

Jesus felt that there were lessons to be learned. The Servant said, "The Sovereign Lord has taught me what to say, so that I can strengthen the weary. Every morning he makes me eager to hear what he is going to teach me."

I don't like to admit it, but the most of what I have learned about God has been, not in the bright sunlight hours of my life, but in the dark midnight hours of pain. Even Jesus learned this way. "Though he was a Son, yet learned he obedience by the things he suffered (Hebrews 5:8)."

A small child often learns best and quickest from being hurt. We say to our children, wanting to spare them any pain,

"Don't touch the stove, it's hot. It will burn the baby." But when we turn our back, baby touches it anyway, and learns from that painful encounter that it is better to obey.

Disobedience has always caused us suffering. We, too, have learned that the hard way. God said to Adam and Eve in Eden, "Don't eat of the fruit of the tree in the midst of the garden." But they disobeyed, took that terrible fall, and that rebellion has caused suffering for the human race ever since.

Sometimes we become angry and resentful at God for telling us what to do. We would like to live our own lives, do our own thing, be independent. We are a bit like the account of the father who said to his son as he left the house on a date with his girl, "Have a good time, son." The boy angrily and belligerently retorted, "Don't tell me what to do!"

Ernest Hemingway wrote, "The world breaks everyone, and afterward many are strong in the broken places." So let us learn from our pain, and become wiser and stronger. Often I have said to God, when the lesson of suffering caused pain so acute it was nearly unbearable, "Lord, whatever you are trying to teach me in all of this, help me to learn it well so that you don't have to do this lesson over again!"

Christ Accepted Suffering Without Rebellion and Resentment — And So Can We

The Suffering Servant witnesses, "I have not rebelled or turned away from him. I bared my back to those who beat me. I didn't stop them when they insulted me, when they pulled out the hairs of my beard and spit in my face."

That must have been hard to do! It is very difficult to accept suffering without complaining, without resentment, without questioning, without anger, without rebellion, without running from it. Yet, Christ our great Example, did not rebel, but humbly, and with total acceptance, endured the pain. The writer of Hebrews describes it, "He humbled himself, and became obedient unto death, even death upon a cross (2:8)."

And again, "For the joy that was set before him, he endured the cross, despised the shame, and is set down at the right hand of the throne of God (Hebrews 12:2)."

Jesus endured all of this patiently. This called for a lot of humility and obedience from our Lord. And now he calls us to "take up the cross, deny self, and follow him" — else we cannot be his disciples. That means submission, self-denial, surrender, and servitude to Christ. Samuel Shoemaker said, "Sooner or later, every Christian must choose between two pains; the pain of a divided mind or the pain of a crucified self."

The kind of obedience that Jesus offered the Father was unhesitatingly given. In the deserts of the Middle East the training of Arabian horses is a grueling process. The trainer requires absolute obedience from the horses. After weeks of putting them through their paces, he gives them a final test. He forces the horses to do without water for a couple of days, then turns them loose within sight of water. Just as they get to the water's edge, ready to plunge in and quench their thirst, he blows the whistle. The horses that come to a complete halt are considered trained and ready for service. They stand their quivering, wanting water desperately, but absolutely obedient. Obedience to the absolute will of God may cause you and me a great deal of pain. C.S. Lewis once wrote, "If you want a religion to make you feel really comfortable, I don't recommend Christianity."

Of this we can be certain: suffering is a fact of life. We will, as surely as we live, know pain: pain of broken relationships, pain of physical hurt, emotional pain, pain of parting by death, pain of misunderstandings, pain of guilt for sin — and we will react to it in some way. We can kick and scream, we can feel sorry for ourselves, we can be angry at God, we can question "Why?" or we can follow Christ with confident trust and endure patiently and obediently.

Christ Trusted In God's Deliverance — So Can We

Isaiah's suffering servant and our Savior believed in ultimate triumph. "But their insults cannot hurt me because the

Sovereign Lord gives me help. I brace myself to endure them. I know that I will not be disgraced. For God is near, and he will prove me innocent. Does anyone dare bring charges against me? Let us go to court together! Let him bring his accusations! The Sovereign Lord himself defends me — who then can prove me guilty?" He knows that deliverance is certain, triumph is sure, victory is ahead — because God is his advocate, as he is also ours.

Dr. Reynolds Greene told of a time when Dr. E. Stanley Jones was preaching for him. He was then 83 years old. He said, "The next 10 years are going to be the greatest I have ever had!" Then, as the congregation looked at the feeble old man standing before them, he continued, with a twinkle in his eye, "I didn't say 'where' they were going to be — but here or there — they will be the greatest with Christ!" That's the way the future can always look to the Christian. The Word says, "The path of the just is as a shining light that shineth brighter and brighter unto the perfect day." Because of whose we are, the future is bright with promise and hope.

Many of us mortals worry ourselves almost to death about things that never happen. We borrow trouble even when we have no trouble. We tend to think negatively. Oz Fitzgerald, a rural mail carrier, once told of the worries of a near relative of his. The old lady said to him, "We got enough meat in the smokehouse to last this year. We got enough hogs in the pen for another year. We got enough shoats running in the pasture for another year. We got enough little pigs coming on for another year. But only the Good Lord knows what we're going to do then!" Jesus had an unshakable confidence in God, for he knew that God would not abandon him to his suffering, so he was obedient to his calling. Nor will God abandon you and me in our hour of trial, pain, and hurt. Christ goes down into the very shadow of death with us. As he is with us on the mountain, so in our low places, the Death Valley of the soul, he is there! Often our suffering and our triumph, our joy and our sorrow, are very close together. The highest point in the United States and the lowest are only a little way apart. Mount Whitney in California, almost 14,500 feet high, is very near Death Valley, 282 feet below sea level. Both are only a few minutes from each other by plane.

A man tells of living and working on Guam. While he was there, it was necessary for him to call Maryland from his office occasionally. Because of the time difference, when he placed a call on Friday at 7 a.m. Guam time, it was still 4 p.m. on Thursday in Maryland. He said that once he was just beginning what promised to be a very trying day at work, when his mood instantly changed for the better when he heard a cheerful voice from Maryland exclaim, "Thanks for calling. I always like talking to someone on Guam. It lets me know that there will be a tomorrow." That's what the Christian can realize during the suffering times — there will be a tomorrow, there will be a sunrise, there will be a triumph. God is always working things out for our good, our victory is just around the corner. Oswald Chambers wrote in one of his devotionals, "Nothing touches our lives but it is God himself speaking." Isn't that a wondrous reminder?

Thomas Ken was a bishop in the Anglican Church, but is not remembered for that. He was once chaplain to Princess Mary at The Hague, but he is not remembered for that. He was once imprisoned in the Tower of London, but he is not remembered for that. He is remembered for four simple, great lines he wrote. They formed the last verse of his *Morning Hymn*. Later, they were in his *Evening Hymn*. Then he composed *Midnight Hymn*, and they are in that, as well. They are familiar to every Christian in the English speaking world. We sing them at nearly every worship service:

> *Praise God from whom all blessings flow!*
> *Praise Him all creatures here below;*
> *Praise Him above ye heavenly host!*
> *Praise Father, Son, and Holy Ghost!*

Our Suffering Servant, our Savior, died in horrible, terrible pain on the cross. But his was the ultimate triumph when God raised him from the dead on Easter Day! We may not know when or how God will deliver us, but we do know that he will. The Psalmist reminds us, "Weeping may endure for the night, but joy comes in the morning." You can count on it!

Maundy Thursday
Jeremiah 31:31-34

Fresh Bread And New Wine

Stories of holy communion events abound. Someone has said that the difference between a Lutheran and a United Methodist is that a Lutheran uses real wine and a United Methodist uses real bread. It is true that Lutherans use real wine and United Methodists seem to feel that Jesus turned the water at Cana into Welch's grape juice; that Lutherans use the small, round pressed wafer and the United Methodists often use a loaf of bread.

But, whatever sort of bread and wine is used, it is still a momentous occasion. On a visit to Jerusalem, I stood in an upper room much like the one that Jesus and his disciples used. Could it have been the same place, I wondered, where on that Thursday evening long ago they partook of that first last supper? Those present must never have forgotten the occasion. In retrospect, years later, it was likely still rife with memories that comforted and convicted. "Lord, is it I who will betray you?" Didn't each disciple there wonder if that weakness were not hidden in some recess of his soul, as it was in Judas? "Take and eat in remembrance of me." Remembrance, oh, yes, they will remember. Can they ever forget that night? "This is my body, this is my blood — drink all of it. This is my blood of the covenant, which is poured out for many for the forgiveness of sins." So this is the new covenant about which Jeremiah spoke! We never realized at the time how glorious it would be!

And, as I stood there, recalling what Scripture told us about the event; I, too, thought and remembered and examined and bowed in awe that such simple elements — bread and wine — could mean so eternally much to such a sinful soul as I!

Jeremiah, in this text, speaks of a new covenant. It will be a unique relationship in which God will bind himself to his people, to be fulfilled by Christ. When Jesus invited his disciples to the table, when he blessed the food, broke the bread and shared the cup, the Lord's supper began. Before it had been only a Passover meal. Now it is more; it is a vivid, visible sign of God saying to those first Christians, and now to us, what he had said to Jeremiah: "I will be their God, and they shall be my people."

This new covenant was ratified in Jesus' death on the cross. There his own precious body was given to become food and sustenance for us, his blessed blood was shed for the forgiveness of sins, for our very life!

Thus it is that on this Maundy Thursday we gather at our Lord's table and drink new wine and eat fresh bread!

Fresh Bread

Two or three times a year, a family member makes several loaves of fresh, wonderful, homemade bread. It is made from a "starter," and anyone who understands bread-making knows it isn't always convenient to make bread every week, but if you don't, your starter will die. This bread, is, in my opinion, the best bread I have ever eaten. Of course, there are lots of wonderful breads: another family member makes mouth-watering poppy-seed bread. Another makes out-of-this-world Danish breakfast bread. My mother made biscuits that would melt in your mouth. And there are other favorites: the shortbread of Scotland, the scone of England, the dark rye of Germany, the hard, crusty roll of France, the tortilla of Mexico, the sour dough of San Francisco. But there is only one bread for the whole human race. Sometimes we sing the communion hymn, "Bread of the World, in Mercy Broken." We eat it at communion, the unleavened bread, Bread for the world, the body of our Lord Jesus Christ.

We all need bread. It is called the staff of life, for it gives sustenance, nourishment, and strength. As we feed on Christ, his body broken for us, we are amazed at the spiritual vigor that comes to us.

Modern diets demand that we delete some things from our eating in order to be healthier or thinner. But the Divine Diet calls for us to partake of Christ, the Living Bread. If we fail to feed on him in our hearts, we become weak, feeble, frail, and sicken and die. We would wisely heed the invitation of the hymn which calls, "Let Us Break Bread Together on Our Knees."

We had dinner in a restaurant once and they served no bread. When we asked if it were not available we were told, "Of course! But our policy here is that we serve bread only upon request." That is the way Christ is offered to us, as well. He is Bread for the world, but only if he is requested. Christ died for all, but he does not force himself on any. His life is not automatically given. We must in repentance and faith ask for it, beseeching the Father, "O give us of that Living Bread that we hunger no more!"

New Wine

The Old Testament sets forth an old covenant, the covenant of the law. It was sealed in the blood of slain animals, usually a lamb. But this covenant had failed. Mankind kept breaking the law of God. What humanity needed was not a new law, but a new heart. So Jeremiah spoke of this, "I will put my law in their minds and write it on their hearts. I will be their God, and they will be my people." What the law could not do, Christ came to do! God, in sending Jesus, gave us a covenant of grace, ratified again in blood — but this time not the blood of animals, but of his own Son, not the blood of a lamb, but of The Lamb.

And this covenant repeats itself each time we read the words of institution of the Lord's supper. His atoning death on the cross is remembered as "the new covenant in my blood." The emphasis is upon atonement; the means of our life and forgiveness is blood. We are saved and made one with God by the shedding of the blood of the crucified Christ.

I learned of a husband and wife who have each donated nearly 20 gallons of blood in their lifetimes. That's 160 pints of blood each! I could not help but speculate on how many lives might have been saved through the unselfish giving of their blood. It was a beautiful gift from one human for other humans — given a pint at a time. But the greatest Donor of all time sweat great drops of his blood in the Garden of Gethsemane, then spilled the rest of it on Calvary's cross-tree. And that blood, applied in repentance and faith, gives us pardon and everlasting life!

A woman once said to me, after we had sung "There Is a Fountain Filled With Blood" in a worship service, "I don't like that song or any other song that has to do with blood. I wish they'd taken them all out of our hymnal. It is unpleasant, ugly, and gory." Blood is ugly and gory, but it is the greatest liquid substance in the world for giving life. As water is essential for physical life, so blood is essential for eternal life.

The Scriptures make it clear, both in the Old and New Testaments, that blood is vital. The Word says, "Without the shedding of blood, there is no remission of sins," "The life is in the blood," "We have redemption through his blood," "We are brought near to God by the blood," "The church was bought with his blood." Without Christ, our Divine Donor, we would be yet in our sins, estranged from God, without forgiveness, without hope, without peace, and dying in our lostness. The writers of the hymns and gospel songs have recognized the primary importance of the blood, so they have written, "Jesus, Thy Blood and Righteousness," "Saved By the Blood of the Crucified One," "There is Power in the Blood," "Nothing But the Blood," and many, many more.

So, on this Maundy Thursday, remembering our Lord, we return again to that upper chamber and hear him say, "This is my blood of the new covenant, poured out for many for the forgiveness of sins." In these hours before Good Friday, let us come kneeling in true repentance and faith, confessing our sins and unworthiness, and with trembling, trusting hands reach out to receive from our Lord, fresh bread and new wine — and leave this place knowing we have been given sustenance and salvation!

Good Friday
Isaiah 52:13—53:1-12

The S & L That Didn't Fail!

A *Peanuts* cartoon strip shows Charlie Brown and Linus as they summarize their team's baseball season. They report that in 12 games they almost scored a run. In right field Lucy almost caught three balls, and once she almost made the right play. They decided between them that they led the league in "almosts." We Christians do not have an "almost" Savior. We have a Lord who saves to the uttermost. He did not and he cannot fail.

At this writing, according to the experts, losses from savings and loans (S & Ls) that have failed now have burgeoned to somewhere in the vicinity of $325 billion, and could hit $500 billion. Taxpayers, of course, will bear the burden of bailout. It has been described as "the worst financial scandal in American history." It remains to be seen if the nation's thrift institution regulator can rid S & Ls of fraud. It is fair to say that, beyond a doubt, S & Ls have failed the American people.

But Christians have a divine S & L that did not and cannot let us down. Earlier in his book, Isaiah speaks of God as the Sovereign Lord, and now the Sovereign Lord, S & L, takes on the identity, in this text, of the suffering servant. This poem was perhaps written, originally, to describe the nation of Israel. John R. W. Stott, in his comprehensive work, *The Cross of Christ*, says, "It seems to be definite, beyond doubt, that Jesus applied Isaiah 53 to himself and that he understood his death in the light of it as a sin-bearing death."

Peter, Paul, Matthew, Luke, and John — the major contributors to the New Testament — together allude to at least eight of the 12 verses of Isaiah 53, ascribing them to Christ's vicarious suffering and penal substitution.

Joachim Jeremias has written, "No other passage from the Old Testament was as important to the church as Isaiah 53."

So when we examine this passage, seeing it amazingly and accurately describing the agonizing atonement of Jesus Christ on the cross, we immediately sense that here we have a Sovereign Lord (S & L) that did not fail!

The Sovereign Lord becomes our suffering Lord, and by his death is redeeming hundreds of thousands who have been enslaved by sin, and is setting them free from bondage and making them candidates for heaven, through faith in his name.

Look with me, at what our never-failing S & L has done:

Our Sovereign Lord Becomes A Servant

God the Father introduces God the Son as his "servant." It is almost incomprehensible that the Sovereign Lord, Creator of heaven and earth, would condescend to take up his abode with us. He will leave the high habitation of heaven to descend to the low living of earth. In heaven he is seated in honor, glory, majesty, power and might; adored and worshiped by angels and archangels. On earth, which is but his footstool, he will be a homeless wanderer, unacclaimed for the most part, ignored, insulted, rejected, reviled, maligned, and mistreated. And of this One, God is saying, "Behold, my servant." The Master is becoming a servant!" How could our Sovereign Lord become a servant for us; why would he?

John the Baptist said of Jesus, "I am not good enough to even untie his sandals." We should be bowing before him; acknowledging his greatness and glory, and yet, with gracious self-debasement the Infinite becomes an infant, the King of Heaven becomes a babe in Bethlehem's barn. His first home was heaven, his next was a stable. His first address was "The Holy City," he grew up in Nazareth, a little obscure village. He who had been served by heaven's hosts announced that "He came not to be served, but to serve, and to give his life as a ransom for many (Matthew 20:28)." He was rich and for our sakes became poor. Angels and archangels fell at his feet, but he stooped to wash the dusty feet of his disciples. And he who was the very light of heaven died in darkness at noon-day.

Our Sovereign Lord Becomes A Sacrifice

A Sunday school teacher reported that once she was discussing with her class of three- and four-year-olds how Jesus is always with us. She said, "He is with us even when we cannot see him." One little fellow agreed, saying, "I know he is. He's the one who opens the doors at the supermarket." Obviously the child was mistaken, but Jesus does open doors. This suffering servant, now becoming our sacrifice, will open the doors to life, to hope, to peace, to God. He is offering himself up to death for us, even death on a cross.

Martin Luther once said of the cross, "We carry his very nails in our pockets." We are all sinners. "All we like sheep have gone astray and the Lord has laid on him the iniquity of us all." Until we own up to the first "all" of this verse we cannot profit from the second "all." We each have to face it: the cross shows us what we are; murderers, liars, cheats, thieves, adulterers, jealous, envious, proud, greedy — you name it, we have done it — we are helpless to help ourselves. Yet he bore our sins in his body on the tree.

As bad as the cross was, the journey to it was long and arduous, too. It meant "coming to his own" and not being received. It meant that often his loving deeds would be misunderstood and criticized. They called him the "Friend of sinners," and aren't we glad he was? They taunted, "He saved others; himself he cannot save." Isn't that one of the most priceless things we know? "Never man spake like this man." How right they were. Even in their mocking rejection of him they managed to magnify the majesty of this wondrous S & L. Their deviltry only declared his divinity!

Then there was the betrayal and the denial of his very own disciples. How that must have hurt his heart. They scourged his back and left it open and bleeding like a plowed field. Surely God's suffering Lord will give up on us, and call us all a bad lot, a lost cause, a bad debt unworthy of redemption — but he does not!

There is more: they must mock him longer and proclaim him a king. So they borrow a robe and a reed for a scepter. And there was that crown of thorns that they thrust on his blessed brow on that first Good Friday morning. In their jeers and jests and jokes they decide, after wrapping the robe about his bleeding shoulders that he must have a coronation. But with what will they crown him? They search for something to be twisted into a coronet. They find a branch in someone's garden, or perhaps it grew along a fence row somewhere nearby — true, it's a bit thorny, but so much the better! A crown for Jesus of Nazareth, King of the Jews, the sign over the cross will read. He is King of the Jews, but also King of the gentiles, and soon to be King of the whole world . . . King of kings Lord of lords, forever and forever — only they don't know it yet!

Somehow that thorn-crowned brow brings his suffering home to us in a very personal way. Most of us do not relate well to the scourging, for we have never been flogged with a whip as he was. We have not felt nails driven in hands and feet as he did, but thorns we understand. Everyone has been pricked by a thorn. Even a beautiful rose has sometimes caused us to feel that kind of pain. In passing, we might just note the reasons for thorns being in our world in the first place. Eden's garden had no thorns until we sinned. Then came the curse as a result of our rebellion, "Cursed is the ground for thy sake . . . thorns also and thistles shall it bring forth unto thee (Genesis 3:17-18)." Even nature testifies to our sin, and our wondrous S & L took the sign of the curse of our sin and wore it on his brow.

So far as we know, the great painters are accurate, when they portray Christ dying with the thorns still on his brow, blood running down, mingling with sweat and tears. The Scriptures say his mockers took off the scarlet robe they had put on him, and gave him back his own robe (the seamless robe the soldiers gambled for at the foot of his cross as he was dying). But it seems his forehead remained thorn-crowned; those sharp and pointed, poison-tipped, ugly symbols of our sin, they remained. This is the gospel! Is there anything our sinful world needs to hear more than this: our Sovereign Lord took the curse of our sin and bore it in our place? He who knew no sin is suffering its penalty in our place. He who owed no debt, took ours, and paid it all. The American Savings and Loans will be bailed out by taxpayers, and heavy though that load may be, we can do it. But the heavy load of sin's debt is too much for any of us — or all of us. We simply do not have, nor can we find, resources that will eradicate that terrible debt. We should sing more often,

> *And when before the throne, I stand in him, complete,*
> *Jesus died, my soul to save, my lips shall still repeat.*
> *Jesus paid it all, all to him I owe,*
> *Sin had left a crimson stain, He washed it white as snow.*

As horrible as his journey to the cross is, the magnitude of our crime toward our S & L is just beginning. They will take this Sovereign Lord, this suffering Savior, and nail him to a rough gibbet of shame — a tree he created in the beginning will be used as a cross to bear his body. It overwhelms the mind: the Creator will be nailed to his own creation by those he created! Amid the physical torment, the mental anguish, the ravaging thirst, the ugly sin-load of the world, he will die. If we uttered the awful, awesome truth, we'd cry out in a long, shuddering, agonizing moan of despair; "My God! We have killed him! We mortals have killed God!"

Our Sovereign Lord Becomes A Savior!

But don't give up! Christ's atoning death is purchasing life for us. His shed blood has opened a fountain where our sins are washed away. The devil is defeated and can no longer claim us as his disciples. The Victim on the cross, is, in reality, the Victor. There is a Portuguese proverb which says, "Architects cover their mistakes with creepers, cooks with sauces, and doctors with earth." But our Savior covers our mistakes and our sins with his own precious blood!

United Methodist Evangelist, Rev. Leo Lacey, tells the story of a young boy working with his father, in one of the textile mills of North Carolina. Suddenly, one day, the boy's clothing was caught in the heavy machinery and began slowly pulling him into the claws of certain death. The father saw what was happening, sizing up the situation in a glance, and knew there was not time to run to the control room to shut off the power. So he deliberately placed his own arm in the cog-wheels to jam the machinery. The boy was saved, but the father later died of infection from his severed arm. All the rest of his life the young man wore a red band around his arm. When people inquired as to the reason, he would answer, "That is the mark of my father upon me. It reminds me that I have been died for." Each time we see a cross, we recollect the red-blood of Christ that was shed for us. We have been died for!

We have hanging in our home a marvelously hand-carved cross which was made by an artist in Oberammergau. It is nearly four feet high, and while the cross-wood is lovely, the captivating feature is the exquisitely carved figure of the suffering Lord portrayed in the clarity and pain of his torturous, crucified death. That Christ as Victim has won my heart, my love, my loyalty, and my allegiance. I am keenly aware that I serve him always imperfectly, and often very poorly, but still I own no other Lord before him.

The S & L That Didn't Fail

Yes, the savings and loans have failed us. Man-made institutions have a way of doing that. They come and go, show profit and loss, rise and fall, but our Sovereign Lord continues to build his kingdom. It is firm, sound, and unshakable, as solid as the Rock Christ Jesus upon which it is founded. You can put all of your primary investments in our divine S & L, it will never fail, and will continue to yield ever higher dividends. You get ever-increasing returns on all you give — and much, much more. G. K. Chesterton said of the cross: "That terrible tree which is the death of God and the life of humanity." Right! He's the S & L that didn't and never will fail!

Easter
Acts 10:34-43

Easter — Fact And Fiction!

A *Family Circus* comic strip shows the children of the family on Easter morning. One asks, "Who laid all these eggs?" The reply of another child is, "The Easter Bunny." "Who colored them?" Again the reply, "The Easter Bunny." The first child asks again, "Who gave us the jelly beans?" The reply, "The Easter Bunny." The family is then shown going to church. In church, the minister is preaching, and asks, "They came to the tomb and saw the stone rolled back, 'Who could have done this?'" And the child in the congregation yells out, "The Easter Bunny!"

But that is fiction. History was not split in half by a rabbit! I remember, as many of you do, as a small child, running around the house on Easter morning, searching for the eggs my parents had hidden. I had been told that the Easter Bunny had brought them. There was a basket to put them in; and on a good day I'd find a chocolate rabbit, hard-boiled, colored eggs, multi-colored jelly beans, and larger candy eggs; orange, yellow, green and lavender. Do you remember the lavender eggs always lasted the longest because they tasted so terrible?

Of course, all of this sort of fits in with Easter's origin which can be traced back to pre-Christian cultures. It was associated with the day of the spring equinox, with the goddess of spring and fertility. The rabbits stood for fertility and the eggs symbolized new life. So, as the pagans became Christianized they sort of cross-fertilized with the Christian celebration of the resurrection and gave it the pagan name of Easter. And, oh, how our commercial world profits from that long-ago merger! They make big profits from our holy resurrection day. It is prime-time for the marketing of new clothes, chocolates, candies, eggs, greeting cards, and Easter lilies. And they milk the money to the last drop with sales: pre-Easter sales, Easter sales, post-Easter sales, even final discount, 80% off, Easter sales.

All of this Easter bunny, Easter eggs, Easter clothes, Easter sales may seem like harmless fun, but if it diverts our attention from the central truth of what the resurrection of our Lord is all about, then it is no longer harmless. I have no personal antagonism against a cute, little bunny who lays eggs for children — (Do you suppose they really believe that stuff we tell them?) — but it is life and death business (no pun intended) if we allow the rabbit to eclipse the fact of the resurrection!

Jesus did not die on a cross and rise again so that we could hunt Easter eggs, but rather that we might have eternal life. So let us be clear: The Easter bunny is really a nice, little critter when relegated to his proper place, but don't forget that it is only an illusion. The rabbit is fiction!

The Fact

And then there is the fact: "God raised his Son from the dead!" God's ultimate victory took place on that Sunday morning which followed the terrible, black, Good Friday of three days ago. Listen to the text; "They killed him, but God raised him from the dead."

Five times in this book of Acts Peter said, "You (or they) killed him, but God raised him from the dead!" Paul said it at Antioch, "You killed him, but God raised him from the dead." The resurrection of Jesus is presented as the cornerstone of truth in the early Christian church. The statement that God raised Jesus from the dead appears twelve times in Acts. Paul begins the epistle to the Romans with the fact of Christ's resurrection from the dead, and bases the Christian's new life on the resurrection of Jesus. And Paul declares decisively and in detail that "if Jesus did not rise from the dead, the entire Christian faith is false and we are left without hope."

Only the resurrection can account for the radical change which took place in Christ's disciples; men who had previously been cowards and losers, but now speak with boldness and authority. If we accept the authenticity of the gospel records, then we cannot deny the historical fact of Christ's bodily resurrection. The physical resurrection of Christ is as inseparable from the Christian message as a chicken from chicken soup.

The non-believers have propounded multitudes of ridiculous theories to circumvent this biblical truth, saying: it was not a physical resurrection, but just a spiritual resurrection, Christ did not really die on the cross, he just fainted and was resuscitated in the coolness of the tomb, that the witnesses were psychologically influenced by their fervor.

But it has ever been true that you can't explain miracles, you accept them. Without a doubt the resurrection is a supernatural event, but without apology we proclaim that Christianity is a supernatural religion. God can, and did, and does intervene in human history — not in violation of natural law which he, by the way, created, but by interposing his higher level of supernatural law when he so chooses. A liberal German, Rabbi Peter Levinson, said as he twitted liberal Christians for their lack of faith, "The demythologizers of Easter are sawing off the branch of faith upon which they were sitting. If I believed in Jesus' resurrection, I would be baptized tomorrow!"

Oh, yes, Easter's fact is the glorious resurrection of our Lord! Martin Luther said there was nothing better than this truth. He stated, "The words, 'Christ is risen from the dead' should be well-marked and written in great letters. Each letter should be as large as a town, yea, even as high as heaven and broad as the earth, so that we see nothing, hear nothing, think nothing, know nothing beyond it."

The Fact Feeds Our Faith

So, the rabbit is only an illusion, but the resurrection is our proof of eternal life. And the text continues with the glorious promise that because Christ died and rose again, that "everyone who believes in him receives forgiveness of sins through his name." What a blessed relief! Christ died, Christ rose again, and now redemption's work is done, Christ is vindicated as Conqueror over death, hell, and the grave, and the way for sinners like ourselves is now wide open to God. Is it any wonder that Easter hymnody is sung in a major key; full of life, triumph, victory, joy, celebration, and hope? The battle is over, the night is past, the victory is won, and the songs of triumph resound across the land.

But this glorious fact also feeds our faith when the path we walk is not bright with light. When we feel despair, hopelessness, and can't see our way we can believe that God will take our impossible situations and help us turn them into triumphs. If he could handle death, can he not take care of whatever problem that confronts you today? You see, we know that when you're dead, you're dead! Right? — Right! Unless God comes on the scene. And that's exactly what Peter keeps saying in Acts; "You killed him, but God . . ." "You killed the Lord of Life, but God . . ." "You crucified him, but God . . ." "You executed him, but God . . ." "You hanged him on a tree, but God . . ." "God" did this impossible thing for his Son, don't you see, then, that he longs to do the same for you? After humanity has done his worst, God does his best.

Perhaps you once sang a little chorus that I sang when I was a child. Its words were something like this:

> *Got any rivers you think are uncrossable;*
> *Got any mountains you can't tunnel through?*
> *God specializes in things thought impossible;*
> *He does the things others cannot do.*

Your problem is not bigger than God. God said through the prophet Jeremiah (32:27), "Nothing is too difficult for me." Jesus said, "All things are possible to him who believes (Mark 9:23)."

So, are there some impossibilities you face in your life today? Maybe it is the impossible situation of a marriage that is almost or altogether on the rocks. Maybe a friend has left you disillusioned, or maybe you've hit the bottom financially, or perhaps you're in trouble at school, maybe you need to sell your house and can't find a buyer, maybe you're caught up in a sin that has you bound in its clutches, maybe . . . impossibilities . . . we face them all the time. What a relief to know that God can work out the situation in my life no matter how hopeless it seems to me.

A man tells of walking down the street, and passing the lady who sold flowers. She was old and wrinkled, but her face was alive with joy. As he stopped to buy a flower, the man said, "You certainly look happy this morning." She responded, cheerily, "Why not? Everything is good." The man noticed how shabbily she was dressed, knew she must be very poor, noted how frail she seemed, so he said, "I only meant that you wear your troubles well." She said, "Let me tell you how I do it. When Jesus was crucified on Good Friday, that was the worst day for the whole world. Then, three days later — Easter — he rose again. So, when I get troubles, I've learned to wait three days. Somehow everything gets all right again." The man related, "She smiled at me as she waved good-bye. Her words still follow me whenever I think I have troubles. I 'wait three days.' "

The God of the impossible has a way, in his own time, of bringing hope out of our hopelessness and life out of our death. I don't think I can ever forget the sad, seeming finality of the words of the text, "You killed him" — but after three days the impossible was made possible, and the rest of the text resounds with victory, "But God — but God raised him from the dead!"

Bill and Gloria Gaither were right on target when they wrote in their song,

> *Because He lives, I can face tomorrow,*
> *Because He lives, all fear is gone;*
> *Because I know He holds the future,*
> *And life is worth the living just because He lives!*

That's the glorious fact of Easter's resurrection!

Easter 2
Acts 5:27-32

Obedience Is An Ugly Word!

A man, bragging on his dog, said, "He's a fine dog. He's so smart, and obedient, too. Why, all I have to do is tell him what to do and he either does it, or he doesn't!" The gospel's success or failure all hinges upon our acceptance or rejection of the word "Obedience."

If we truly have faith, we will obey God. Obedience implies that we are not independent, that we are accountable to another, that we do have someone over us, that there is a higher authority than ourselves.

In a world where we are taught that it is our "right" to do "our own thing," "be our own person," do it because it "feels good" — we find that God expects us to lay all that aside and obey him! Just how radical can you be?

Naturally we all conform to others when we must. We won't speed too much above the limit lest we get caught and have to pay a fine, we won't lie, steal, and cheat unless we can get by with it. But give us a chance and we give ourselves permission to do as we please. A television commercial advertising for Burger King encourages the same kind of disobedience by saying, "Sometimes you've gotta break the rules!" After all, rules are made to be broken. The truth is, for many folks, obedience is an ugly word. We don't like it and will only put up with it if we have to. So, when we are forced into it, we give token obedience to parents, bosses, the law, the "higher authorities," but willing obedience is a rarity. After all, who wants to conform to someone else's ideas, commands, orders? Children can hardly wait to come "of age," so they can do as they please. Wives plead for equality which will free them from submission to husbands. We long for promotions in the work force, then we will give the orders and show "how it ought to be done."

A woman asked her pastor. "Will you please tell me what your idea of obedience is?" Holding out a blank sheet of paper, the pastor replied, "It is to sign your name at the bottom of this blank sheet, and let God fill it in as God wills." He was right. Obedience is to bow to the Lordship of Jesus Christ. You cannot make Christ the king of your life until you abdicate. Kierkegaard claims, "To be fully obedient we must hold onto nothing, and surrender ourselves totally to the promptings of God's Spirit."

This total, absolute, and willing obedience becomes the crucial and critical issue in this text. The fuller narrative is an account of some of the events which took place in the beginnings of the new church which was brought into being after the resurrection of Jesus. You will note that the history of the early Christian church is rife with solid evidence that wherever the obedient disciples went they were sure to find three things — always these three things: and the first is . . .

They Had Power

Our first glimpse of the apostles (we are not told how many, or which ones specifically, but they seem to be led by Peter) finds them busy at doing exactly what God had told them to do and great and powerful events followed in their train. They were teaching and preaching in the name of Jesus. They performed miracles in Jesus' name. They healed the sick in Jesus' name. They exorcised evil spirits in Jesus' name. Even the dead came to life! All very powerful results followed their obedience.

A man asked his friend to come to a revival. His little girl, overhearing the invitation, asked, "Daddy, what's a revival?" He said, "Let's go look it up in the dictionary." They found that it said, "To bring to life again." The child began to jump up and down in excitement and said, "Oh, goody! Daddy, let's go! We'll get to see some dead people raised!" I wonder if that would not be the actual fact if more of us gave full obedience to God during periods of revival?

The obedient commitment, arising out of the apostles' conviction about Christ, resulted in marvelous things in their ministry. They were fully aware that they did not go it alone, they recognized the Holy Spirit as their colleague, the One who worked with them. The record reads, "And so is also the Holy Spirit, whom God hath given to them that obey him." You see, the witness we make for Christ is always a mutual witness. I cannot be a witness without the help of the Holy Spirit. And the Spirit, in turn, limits himself, for he will not be a witness except through you and me — obedient disciples of his. It has to be by cooperation. Absolute obedience on our part is a necessity. If we find we are powerless disciples, could it be that we are trying to do it all alone? Your witness and my witness, by itself, is never enough, but our witness cannot fail if it be the Holy Spirit witnessing in and through us with his mighty power. When God is at work in obedient men and women you can count on it — you will have power, but you will also find the second of the three things I mentioned earlier . . .

They Had Trouble

Just because we are obedient, that of itself is no indication that God is insulating us against the hard knocks of life. Everything is not always rosy. Reminds me of the Irish comedian, Hal Roach. He told of a doctor who came into the hospital and said to his patient, "We have bad news and very bad news for you. The bad news is that you only have 24 hours to live." The patient inquired, "What is the very bad news?" The doctor replied, "We should have told you yesterday."

It's not always that difficult, but anyone who decides to be fully obedient to the gospel mandate may as well know there will be some trouble. The devil will see to it. You can't invade his territory without a terrible fight from him. The name of Christ and the God of this world have always been — and always will be — at odds with each other. There is a real power of evil, and evil will not easily submit to the power of God invading his domain, certainly not without a fight!

The jealousy of the high priest and his associates who were members of the Sanhedrin prompted them to have the apostles arrested and jailed for teaching and preaching in the name of Jesus. When they were brought before the Sanhedrin to be questioned by the high priest, he said, "We gave you strict orders not to teach in this Name, yet you have filled Jerusalem with your teaching."

The conflict of authority now begins. Peter and the apostles answered their accusers with irrefutable logic, "We ought to obey God rather than men." In other words, "You told us not to preach in this Name, the Spirit told us to preach in this Name, so, who is the higher authority? What possible option did we have, to obey God or you? The angel of God said, 'Speak!' The rulers of the city said, 'Speak not!'" The powers that be are ordained of God, and generally it is our Christian duty to obey them; but there may be times when the higher authority of our God demands obedience in defiance of lesser human authorities. "We must obey God," they said. That was their commitment, and should be ours. We must! After all, who were Annas and Caiaphas, and the whole lot of all those impressive dignitaries, to men whom Christ had bidden to speak and to whom he had given the Spirit of the Father to speak in and through them?

The apostles were not anti-authority, they understood obedience to those in power, they were not stupid; but the pivotal issue was whose authority? Obedience to whom? And for them, God had the final word. God was the supreme authority. They would gladly bow to human authority until it clashed with divine authority, and then the choice must be God.

So, now they are in trouble, and will get in yet more trouble, for the Sanhedrin were not too happy with Peter's reason for obeying God. He said, "You killed Jesus by hanging him on a tree, but God raised him from the dead." What marvelous convictions Peter had! The Jesus whom they killed by crucifixion is risen, is ascended, is reigning, and is saving. What a word for days such as these! Our Savior, whom governments ignore, whom the media ignores or casts aspersions upon, whom many disdain, is on the throne of the universe in glory; "Him hath God exalted to his right hand to be Ruler." What glorious good news we have; from that throne he saves repentant sinners. His sovereign gift is salvation, "To give repentance and forgiveness of sins." And praise be his name, the risen Lord still has authority on earth to forgive sins! And only he can!

But this good news is not accepted as good news by everyone. These men were furious and wanted to have the apostles put to death. Why wouldn't they? They killed Jesus, now they'll kill his followers. Yes, we'll have some problems if we walk with obedience to our Lord. Not everyone will like us and talk about how nice we are. Sometimes, in spite of all we can do, things will go awry. Where did we ever get the distorted notion that we, as Christians, have a right for things to always go well for us? Why would we expect life to be a bed of roses without thorns, why would we expect to have no sickness or pain for ourselves or our loved ones, why expect that those who are dear and near to us will never die, why would we expect no burglars would ever steal our property, why would we expect to have no insoluble problems? We can't expect everyone to laud and love and accept and understand us. We can't expect affirmation for all our actions, even when they were motivated by love and obedience.

It didn't happen to those early disciples, and it won't happen to us. But wait! An advocate for these men came from an unexpected qurter. Gamaliel, a Pharisee, a teacher of the law, spoke up and addressed the court and said, "I advise you to leave these men alone. Let them go. If their purpose and activity is of human origin it will fail. But if it is from God, you will not be able to stop these men, you will only find yourselves fighting against God." Did you get that? Even Gamaliel realized that you can't stop men and women who are obeying God!

Gamaliel's logic prevailed, and so the court had the apostles flogged (beaten with the Jewish penalty of "40 stripes save one"), and after they had received the 39 lashes of terrible beating (the Sanhedrin just couldn't resist one further show of their authority), they ordered them to speak no more in the Name of Jesus, and let them go free. (What an utterly wasted warning to men who were fully committed to obedience to God!)

If we are tempted to feel pretty "holy and self-righteous" in our attempts at full obedience, we might do well to know that things can still occasionally go wrong. I like the story that is told of the nearly 500 passengers who were seated in the California Bullet Train as the inaugural journey got underway. As the train left San Francisco and began speeding through tunnels and over bridges along the San Andreas fault, an assuring voice came over the public address system: "Ladies and gentlemen; there is no crew on this train, but there is nothing to worry about. This entire system is fully computerized and automated, it represents the latest developments in modern technology. You will be transported to southern California at speeds in excess of 200 miles per hour in perfect safety. Every single operation has been tested, re-tested, and tested again. Be assured that there is not the slightest chance that anything can go wrong . . . can go wrong . . . go wrong . . . go wrong . . . wrong . . . wrong . . ." Yes, sometimes things will go wrong, and you may well pay some pretty high prices to be obedient to God. But, before I make it sound too difficult, and before I talk you out of this required obedience, let me remind you of the other certainty of obedience. Always with the promised power and the possible trouble, you will find . . .

They Had Joy!

When the apostles had been arrested and jailed, an amazing thing happened. The angel of the Lord came and opened the prison doors for them that night, and encouraged them to "Go and tell the full message of this new life." Had they had no troubles, there would have been no angel! And so, now free men, they start again to preach at daybreak. It must be that when an angel sets you free from jail you want to get an early start on whatever it is you are told to do! So, daybreak finds them obeying again.

The very idea of persecution makes most of us shudder, but Christ disagreed. Persecution is a priceless privilege that should make us leap for joy when it is done for righteousness' sake (Luke 6:22-23). Somewhere along the way we have felt the constant need to be on a happy high all the time. Don't forget that Christians are not the only ones who are happy. For some people, things make them happy; a new home, new car, boat, jewelry, prestige, and power. We Christians are never promised happiness, but rather joy. Joy is that inner delight, that quiet satisfaction that abundance of possessions or lack of them, that praise of others or lack of it, does not affect.

If we remember that the Holy Spirit is given to those who are obedient, and that one of the evidences of his presence is joy, then we know that the outer facts, be they good or evil, cannot interrupt nor destroy Christian joy.

A delightful story is told in *The Little Flowers of St. Francis* about Francis teaching Brother Leo the meaning of perfect joy. As the two walked together in the rain and bitter cold, Francis reminded Leo of all the things that the world, including the religious world, believed would bring joy, adding each time, "Perfect joy is not like that." Finally, in exasperation Brother Leo asked, "I beg you in God's name to tell me where perfect joy is!" Whereupon Francis began enumerating the most humiliating, self-abasing things he could imagine, adding each time, "O Brother Leo, write that perfect joy is there." These words are hard for us to deal with today, and yet, it is said that it was not until St. Francis gave himself up to God, silver and soul, that he started singing and dancing in the streets. Christian joy is really never complete until we surrender ourselves unconditionally to obeying God.

When the apostles left the court, were they weeping and groaning and crying with pain from the flogging they had received? No. Were they grumbling that God had let them down when what they were doing was his will? No. Did they bow, then, to the threats of the Sanhedrin and cease their preaching? No. They left the court rejoicing — that's right, rejoicing — because they had been counted worthy of suffering disgrace for the Name. Does that not make us feel shameful when we have been silent lest we be laughed at, or called demented, or labeled as religious radicals? Day after day the apostles went from house to house and in the courts; they never stopped teaching and preaching the good news that Jesus is the Christ. If the church of today could get back to that kind of obedience, there would again be record numbers coming to own Christ as Lord, people would repent of their sins and believe and be baptized, and the kingdom would expand — but the bottom line is always obedience.

The kind of irrepressible joy which the apostles had has been experienced by others who have known also the commitment of obedience, have felt the power, have endured the trouble, and found the joy. History records that the apostle John, who led Polycarp to Christ, had warned him that suffering might follow, but as the years passed, Polycarp managed to escape serious persecution. He became bishop of Smyrna, and he became the leading Christian figure in Asia. But at 86 years of age, a Roman proconsul ordered some Christians thrown to the lions to provide amusement, and decided to include Polycarp. The crowd exploded with shouts and calls when they saw him led into the area. "Curse Christ!" the proconsul ordered, and Polycarp's reply was eloquent in its simplicity. "Eighty-six years I have served him, and he never did me wrong. How can I blaspheme my King, who saved me?" And he died at the stake, one of the early Christian martyrs, but with joy in his soul.

It was certainly not a life without struggle and trouble and persecution for Martin Luther, but his life of obedience is one of great joy. John Wesley, for all of his struggles, his being misunderstood by the church he loved, after living a life of zeal and fervor, died, saying, "Best of all, God is with us."

My own mother's Christian journey was an example of all I've said here. She was poor most of her life, she brought 10 children into the world, she knew cold, hunger, poverty, exhaustion, and finally, after suffering a long time, succumbed to cancer. But she lived one of the most victorious, vibrant, Christian examples I have known. In spite of all the pain and struggle she had a joy that could not be extinguished by outer circumstances. She sang the great hymns of the church and the gospel songs almost constantly. I recall one evening when she was preparing the evening meal, dad was also in the kitchen, trying to read the evening paper, and mother kept interrupting him by talking to him. Finally, tired of the intrusion on his concentration, dad said, "Janie, I wish you'd be quiet! I'm trying to think." Mother didn't say a word in return, for she really was sorry to have bothered him. But with her next breath, without malice or intent, she broke into singing, for that's what she did most of the time anyway. Somehow it was hilariously appropriate that she inadvertently chose the lines from the hymn, "Redeemed," which says, "I think of my blessed Redeemer, I think of him all the day long, I sing for I cannot be silent, His love is the theme of my song." Yes, I've known her in lots of trouble, but never without that spark of joy that springs up eternally in the heart that walks in faith and obedience.

Obedience Is The Key

Is there anything we Christians of today need more than an uncompromising, unreserved, continuous obedience to our Lord? This is one of the conditions of being filled with the Holy Spirit. Would you know this mighty power of love mastering you, using you, sustaining you, and glorifying Christ through you? Then obey! Obey! Maybe obedience is not such an ugly word after all!

Easter 3
Acts 9:1-20

"Because Of You," Or "In Spite Of You?"

Saul's conversion is important to us because we are always wanting detailed accounts of the journey of those people who have become great or famous. They always fascinate us. We avidly consume all the minute specifics we can find about them, sometimes even stooping to seek out tidbits of gossip. We are titillated by the trivial. Why was Sir Winston Churchill buried in a small country cemetery rather than in Westminster Abbey? Why was Churchill born in the servant's quarters of Blenheim Palace rather than in the upstairs rooms reserved for dignitaries? Did Franklin D. Roosevelt have a mistress and did John F. Kennedy have extramarital affairs? Has the passion gone from the marriage of Prince Charles and Princess Di? Will Elizabeth Taylor marry yet again? Insatiable is our appetite for singularities in noteworthy people. So, since we know how vastly important Saul is to our Christian faith, we latch onto Luke's accounts with ready interest. Let us be aware that this is the first of three accounts of the conversion of Saul (Acts 9, 22, and 26). Only an event of greatest import would ever cause Luke, who is usually known for his brevity and concision, to repeat it so often.

But even more than our interest in important people, we are desirous of knowing about Saul because of what conversion is and how it occurs. We realize that nothing is more staggering than knowing salvation through faith in Christ, so we read of this man's pilgrimage with keen interest, for we want to know, too: "What must I do to be saved?" "How can I be right with God?" "Is there a clue here that will help me to be converted, and to help others come to faith?"

So, let us use Saul's experience to guide us in our attempt to find Christ and then to assist others to become followers of the Way. The Way, people of Christ — that's the description of the Christian faith and its adherents, used a number of times in Acts, even before they were called Christians. This term was not always meant as a term of approbation to be called of the Way. Often it was a slur against the believer in Christ, for the pagan priests were convinced that the Christian way was a way of heresy. Later, Paul was to say to Felix, "I do admit this to you: I worship the God of our ancestors by following that Way which they say is false (Acts 24:14)." But the term certainly was not always uncomplimentary, for it did mean something special. It said that the Christians had a special walk, or manner or life. How wonderful to be accused of walking after a certain way so that your detractors would be reminded of Jesus! So closely did they pattern their lives after Christ that they could be distinguished by it. It's true that often today we are recognized by our creed — Arian, Athanasian, or Pelagian, or by our ceremonies and how we perform them — baptism by sprinkling or immersion, or by our divisions — liberal or conservative, but tragic that we rarely are marked by our way of living, acting, talking, and thinking. Far too seldom do we hear it said, "Now that person is a Christian!"

So how did Saul become a true follower of the Way? How did his conversion come about? We need to know how his decisive encounter with the Way himself (for our Lord's own claim was "I am the Way") came about.

The Conversion

When first we meet Saul of Tarsus we know him to be an almost fanatical persecutor of those of the Way. We know he had witnessed the martyrdom of Stephen and then had gone on a personal crusade against Christians in Jerusalem, invading the privacy of their homes and hauling them away to prison. After ravaging Jerusalem, he is still looking for more ways to vent his anger against this new sect which was born out of the life and death of that man called Jesus. Jesus, whom they had killed by hanging on a tree. They crucified him, now it is Saul's bounden duty to stamp out his followers — all of them — by whatever means it takes.

So, learning that many of the Jesus people had scattered to Damascus, Saul obtained orders from the chief priest to continue his murderous, merciless mission there. In true vigilante fashion he takes his letters of authorization and begins to extend his persecution all the way to Damascus.

Damascus is 150 miles from Jerusalem and he is nearing his destination when he is confronted with someone with a greater plan. The same Lord who had exposed him to the vital faith of the church, to the soul-searching experience of watching Stephen die with words of forgiveness on his lips for his killers, now begins to draw the net around Saul.

It takes four to six days to get to Damascus from Jerusalem. What do you suppose Saul thought about enroute? A man of Saul's intelligence and learning had to think and remember and wonder about these strange Jesus people. What made them tick? Who was right? Could this Jesus have been the promised Messiah? What made these folks love Jesus to the death? Why did they make him so furious? What did he care what they did if he, Saul, were right? What made their lives so different? Did these questions occur to him?

Of course, we never know what people are thinking, no matter what they say. On our tour to the United Kingdom I met a man who told me he was an atheist. I learned that he was an exceptionally fine historian, and that he had taught for years at one of our outstanding universities. In a breakfast conversation he said, rather condescendingly, to me, "I don't believe in God. I don't believe in life after death. When you tell me that knowing Christ is a matter of faith, I say, 'the mind cannot accept what cannot be proven.' I think you are wrong in your confidence in Christ now and in your hope for heaven later. What do you say to that?" I responded,

"You are right about this one thing; I can't prove it. Faith is a matter of the heart more than the head, and reason is often the enemy of faith. But, even if I am wrong — and I'm sure I'm not — and you are right, I have more to smile about than you. I have hope even when things seem hopeless, and I am not shattered at the thought of death, for I look to a brighter future. The fact is, right now, I'm happier in my faith than you are without faith!" He smiled and said, "Well, that much I do admit." And the rest of the trip he dogged my heels for further conversation. I tell you, you just never know what someone is thinking and feeling, regardless of what their actions say.

But now Saul is on his way — almost there — when suddenly, at high noon, a bright light flashed, so brilliant in intensity that he and his companions were thrown to the ground. The light is followed by a voice telling him that he is an enemy of God, engaged in warfare against God's own people. When Saul asks for the voice's I.D., the speaker identifies himself as Jesus. Then the Lord instructs Saul to go into the city where he will be told what to do. The one who is used to giving orders is now receiving them. Saul, likely shaking with fear and awe, proceeds to obey the voice, but when he opens his eyes he finds that he cannot see. He is blind! We know that before he will see with his eyes again he will have the eyes of his soul enlightened — and that's the best illumination of all! Saul of Tarsus is about to become Paul the Apostle.

The Conveyors

The Lord reaches each of us differently. We may not all have, and probably won't, so dramatic an encounter as Saul, but the important thing is how we respond to Christ. Saul was brought to the end of his own resources, his own cleverness, learning, and pride — and so must we be. Perhaps the reason so few of us have definite conversion experience is that we have not allowed ourselves to know how deep is our need for a Savior. Only those who are very ill are aware of the need for a physician. We are not doing God a favor to let him save us. He is doing a radical operation of rescuing us from death and hell and the punishment we so surely deserve for our sins. If we only could recognize how dire is our distress, we might also realize how dramatic is our deliverance!

Saul's conversion is not a sudden conversion, but it is a sudden surrender. It's true that the light at midday was a sudden experience, but a lot of factors have gone into this struggle before this time and place.

We do not become Christians in isolation. Think about it — you are a Christian today because of whom? What factors? How many people touched your life on your journey to Christ? I can never say, when someone comes to own Christ as Lord in a revival I am preaching, that "He or she is my convert," for though I may be the one who prays with them, receives their confession of faith, and may baptise them in Christ, still, how many others touched them to bring them to this place of ultimate decision?

Consequently, it is essential that others who are outside of the faith have no difficulty identifying us as Christians. The Irish tell the story of Murphy, who went into a restaurant in New York and said to the man at the counter, "I want a burger, fries, and a chocolate shake." The man replied, "You must be Irish." Murphy said, "I can't believe it. Everybody always knows." He vowed to disguise his Irishness if it's the last thing he did. He went to school to lose his accent. He got a whole new wardrobe. He then went to a finishing school to learn all the proper manners and how always to behave. Then, some months later he went to the same restaurant, and said to the man at the counter, "I would like to start with some vichyssoise, then I'll have steak tartare, and I'll complete the meal with fresh raspberries." The man said, "You must be Irish." Murphy replied, "How is it that you always know I'm Irish?" The man said, "Because this is a hardware store." Just so easy should it be to know us as people of the Way.

Too, it is imperative that we realize our responsibility to be of the Way, rather than in the way. We have all experienced having to say to another, "Please, get out of the way." They have, at the moment, become a hindrance, an obstacle, or a threat to what is being accomplished, so we say they are in the way. But people of the Way should never be in the way of those who need to find Christ. Rather, we are obligated to be persons whose lives are indelibly stamped with the imprint of Jesus. We never know when someone is watching us. Sometimes people become Christians because of us, other times in spite of us. As people of the way, we are an influence whether we want to be or not. Sometimes it is consciously, other times it is unconsciously, but whether accidentally or on purpose, we carry weight either for or against our Lord. Terrifying thought and responsibility, isn't it?

A minister from a Communist party, speaking of churches being allowed to exist in an atheistic society, said, "Christianity is no threat as long as you can contain it to one day a week. It is only when it becomes a way of life that the authorities seek to stamp it out."

If we could manage to be real in all of our lives, it would amount to a powerful inducement for others to come to Christ. A woman in a certain bank said she sees counterfeit money almost every day. When she was asked how she spotted the phoney money, she said, "We learn to spot the fake money by recognizing and handling so much of the real thing. Once you know the real, you can spot the counterfeit in a minute." So it is that the authentic Christian becomes his own validator, and the indicator of the false. The world needs because of believers and fewer in spite of persons.

Paul became a Christian in spite of his rigid, legalistic background, in spite of his prejudices and arrogant opinions, in spite of his learning and cleverness. But because of the seeking Savior and persons of the Way, he was found by Christ. Of course it is always through Christ's initiative that we are apprehended in our head-long dash for self-destruction. Because of Christ, Saul found knowledge of the Way — Way both in a person and in a direction for his life.

We, too, are saved, because God always uses the intricate weaving of other lives into our conversion. There were those persons who became an indispensable part of God's transforming power to make us his own.

Look at some of those of the Way whom God used in this marvelous redemptive work for Saul. There was an obedient-to-God-Ananias who came with a brother's heart to help. There were the people who led him, as he was blind, to Damascus. There was Judas, in whose house he found hospitality. There were the unnamed disciples among whom he spent certain days. There was his revered teacher, Gamaliel, who had been conciliatory to the church. And back of this company, surely, the remembrance of Stephen, who was a witness to the very end, praying for his persecutors, walking as a person of the Way right into death. And how many others do you suppose there were, whose names the Record does not mention? Add them together, with the sweet and compelling intervention of Christ on the Damascus Road, and you have the capitulation of Saul to allow Jesus as Lord in his life!

How different the outcome might have been in this great man's life without these people of the Way — some of them so obscure we don't even know their names. But they were the bridge over whom Saul passed from the old life to the new. It is a sobering thought to know that when a life of great potential fails, it is not the shining light of God which is lacking, for he is always faithful, but a human life who at a critical time might have been "in the way" rather than of the Way.

I, among many others, give thanks to God for the consistency of the life of Billy Graham. There has been a number of evangelistic stars who have ascended in recent years, and many have fallen, as they were beset by scandal, political controversy, or organizational woes. But Billy Graham remains untainted, the most admired religious leader in America, and the most durable. It was 50 or more years ago that a tall, young Billy delivered his first sermon one cold night before a few Baptists in Bostwick, Florida. Since then, he has preached in person to upwards of 100 million people, more than any other clergymen in history, except perhaps Pope John Paul. Billy Graham was quoted in *Time* (Nov. 14, 1988, p. 86) as saying, "From the very beginning of my career I was frightened — I still am — that I would do something to dishonor the Lord." Well, thanks be to God!, so far so good. He continues to be a because of person of the Way.

I can personally witness that I am a Christian today in spite of a deep poverty when I was growing up which made me terribly shy and insecure around others. I was embarrassed because of my poor home, my poor clothes, and my obvious lack of material things. Also, I had a number of friends who thought it was clever to laugh at anyone who claimed the Christian faith. There were some years when my father, crippled by alcoholism and mad at God, refused to have anything to do with the church and badgered me to stay away as well. Then there were those Christians whose example of the Way left much to be desired. I shall never forget one Easter when we had no money for new clothes or new shoes, and because I needed them so badly had nothing to wear to church. My mother made me a dress from a scrap of material, probably meant for herself, and then managed to scrape together enough coins to make a dollar. She knew I was wearing cardboard inside my shoes to keep my feet off the ground for I had such large holes in the soles. She handed me the dollar and said, "Honey, go downtown to the Brokerage (a cheap, discount store) and see if you can find a pair of shoes that cost no more than this." I was so excited, and went shopping for new shoes, and found one pair. Just one pair was all they had in my size. I found them on the dollar-sale-rack, and they were bright red. I'd never had red shoes before, but they seemed wonderful to me. I was delighted to think of getting to wear them to Sunday school and church the next day. But, to this day I still hurt when I remember the pain and embarrassment I felt when I met a woman in the aisle of the church that Sunday, who looked at my feet, and said, "How could you have the nerve to wear red shoes to church? You look like a Jezebel, only harlots wear red shoes!" I was cut to the quick, for not only did I not think there was anything wrong with red shoes, I knew I could not afford others. There was a woman, supposedly of the Way, but that day was definitely in the way of my becoming a Christian. People are Christians in spite of us or because of us.

On the other hand, however, exposure to the Word of God as it was preached, and taught, and lived, meant that the Holy Spirit came to me again and again with entreaty, with wooing urgency, to give my life to Christ. Along with the Spirit's gentle and powerful drawing me like a moth to a flame, there was that network of people of the Way who made so attractive to me the Christian life. There was first and foremost, my Christian mother whose daily singing of hymns as she worked around the home, whose vibrant faith, and whose passionate prayers for her children that were so real I could neither deny nor ignore them. There were those pastors of the church, people of God who preached the Word with love and power and conviction and authority. There was a Sunday school teacher, who really didn't know much about the Bible, and even less about theology (I now know), but who, nonetheless, believed it all, was infinitely patient with my endless questions, and I owe her an unpayable debt. There were those friends whose love for Christ attracted me and enticed me to trust him, too. And then there was that evangelist, Dodson was his name, and he always wore a red tie, who, in a revival, made it so easy for me to come to Christ as he taught me to pray the sinner's prayer, "Lord, be merciful to me a sinner." And, "because of" them and others, I walk as one "of the Way."

Laurence Houseman said, "A saint is one who makes goodness attractive." Many have done that through the ages. May God give us the same initiative. Paul said it so well to Timothy, and it could become our watchword, ". . . Be thou an example of the believers, in word, in conversation, in charity, in spirit, in faith, in purity."

Easter 4
Acts 13:15-16, 26-33, [38-39]

A Word Of Encouragement!

There are a lot of folks around these days who seem to be ready to unload a bit of their discouragement and depression upon you. A man tells that it seemed every time he walked in the door, as he came home from work, his wife would pounce on him with long tales of woe about the day's calamities and problems. Finally, he sat down and talked about it with her. He said that, after some discussion, she agreed that before she hit him with the day's disasters, she would at least let him first sit down and eat his dinner. But the very next evening, as he walked in the door from work, his wife met him at the door as usual. She said, "Honey, hurry up and eat your dinner. I have something terrible to tell you!"

In today's text there is a request for a cheerful word, too. Paul is on his first missionary journey. He and Barnabas have arrived in Pisidian Antioch, a Roman colony that has a large Jewish population. Usually, he went to a synagogue first, when he went to a city to preach. This made sense, for the synagogue provided a ready-made preaching situation with a building, regularly scheduled meetings, and a congregation who already knew the Old Testament Scriptures. It was customary for the leaders of the synagogue to invite visitors to speak, especially if they were visiting rabbis such as Paul. Gathered there, this day, were the Jews who would ordinarily attend such a gathering, and also gentiles who wanted to worship God. They were not Jewish proselytes, but these gentiles believed in one God and respected the moral and religious teaching of the Jews.

So, Paul is invited to speak, but notice that they also told him what the subject matter would be. I wonder what people would ask us preachers to preach about if they were given the opportunity to choose? The leaders addressed Paul and

Barnabas warmly, "Brothers, if you have a word of encouragement, please speak." Note the "if," the invitation implies that it is contingent upon the content of the message.

We Need A Word Of Encouragement

All of us need and want encouragement. No matter how educated we are, how old we are, how self-sufficient we are; we never outgrow our need to be stroked, encouraged, comforted, supported, and invigorated. And yet, encouragement is often a commodity in short supply. An old minister, on his deathbed, was asked, "If you had it all to do over, would you do anything differently?" He replied, "Yes, I would have criticized less and encouraged more."

We live in pretty heavy days. We have a multitude of concerns: personal, inter-personal, national and international. Are we safe from nuclear warfare? Will the Middle East ever know peace? Will South Africa solve its problems? Is the stock market a safe investment? Is there hope for a cure for the AIDS epidemic? Can we ever solve the drug problem? Will I have enough money to send my children to college? Is my job secure? Will my pension/retirement funds be sufficient? Will my wife/husband/children/parents/friends ever understand me? Will I (or my loved ones) survive this threatening illness? What about death; am I ready to die? Am I prepared to meet God?

Oh, yes, it's easy enough to see why these leaders of the synagogue asked for an encouraging word. There are a host of calamity mongers around who say, "It's no use" — "It's a hopeless situation" — "It will never work" — "You're a failure" — "Dummy! How could you be so stupid!" Some people just naturally bring discouragement; like the Scot who said to another Scot, "What a fine day! It's a rare and bonnie morn!" The other replied, "Yes, but we'll suffer for it!"

I often think of the wonderful people who have spoken words of support and encouragement to me in my ministry.

I might have made it without them, but it would have been far, far more difficult. I shall never forget trying to preach a revival in a little town in Missouri. It was my second revival I had ever tried to conduct. I was 19 years old, between my first and second years of college, uneducated in the ministry, very naive, and the only thing I had going for me was that I was positive God had called me to preach and I was excited about trying to do it. I had gone to this little church to preach for one week; Sunday through Sunday. God blessed the services, the people filled the church each night, many came to confess Christ as Savior, and there was a high enthusiasm in the town for the revival. (No thanks to me, there just wasn't anything else going on in the town, and it was sort of a "curiosity" to see and hear a 19-year-old-girl-type-preacher.) At the end of the week, the pastor suggested that since I was not scheduled to be anywhere else the following week, we just continue the services and have a two-week revival. That was fine with me except for one detail; I didn't have any more sermons! And neither did I think I could get seven more sermons that quickly. But the pastor assured me, "Oh, God will help you!" I believed him, which might have been a major mistake, so each day of the second week I desperately prayed and studied for a sermon for that particular night. About Wednesday of the second week I finally found a last-minute text from Amos, "Prepare to meet thy God." I latched onto the theme and tried to think of something to say. I long since had told them all I knew; several times over. It was a bad, bad sermon. Everything conspired, it seemed, to make it a disastrous service. Add to the poor sermon the fact that it was stifling hot and a general restlessness came over the congregation. Bugs flew in the open, unscreened, windows. The congregation was vastly entertained by a cat that meandered up the center aisle of the church and into the pulpit and rubbed against my legs. I picked it up and asked someone to put it outside. Within a couple of minutes the cat returned and this time I vowed to ignore it, but in forgetting it I stepped back on it, and it yowled to high heaven. The congregation was in stitches and I was embarrassed and frustrated, still struggling to persuade the people to "prepare to meet God." Finally it ended and I went to the door as usual, to meet the people as they departed. How I would love to have avoided them all, gone to my room, and suffered in darkness and solitude and silence. But one man was there — he had driven 45 miles to the service, returning home each evening, and had not missed a single night of the revival. He shook my hand and said, "Young lady, that message tonight was the best of all your sermons so far!" Let me tell you, that was an encouraging word. He will never know, until I get to heaven, how much I needed and appreciated his encouragement. It was just the "right" thing to say. Mark Twain once remarked, "The difference between the right word and the almost right word is the difference between lightning and the lightning bug."

We all need an encouraging word! And so, in response to the request in the synagogue, Paul stood up and said, "Listen to me!" — and he begins his sermon. He started with the Old Testament Scriptures which he was sure they knew, and he focused on the reign of David and David's special place in God's affections. He then makes the claim that Jesus, a direct descendant of David, is the fulfillment of God's promise to Israel to send a Savior. He also reminds them that they had killed him. Even while God was graciously keeping his promise to them, they condemned his Son Jesus and put him to death on a tree. Without any proper grounds for a death sentence, they asked Pilate to execute Jesus. And after they had crucified him, they buried him. Now, of course, it was true that these particular Jews and gentiles had not been the ones who had actually crucified Jesus. That had been carried out by the people in Jerusalem. Still, all of them carried the stigma of unbelief and failure to recognize and receive the Son of God that had been sent.

It doesn't sound like an encouraging word from Paul, yet, does it? But you cannot give a true word of encouragement until you've faced the facts as they are, and then looked to see if there can be found any reason for hope and cheer. A blind optimism that is based on a non-reality is no help at all. If we are to have permanent and real refreshment and encouragement, it must come from looking at the hard facts, assessing the situation, and see if there is a way out of the dilemma.

The Best Word Of Encouragement Is Forgiveness

Now Paul comes to the good news, that "word of encouragement" they had asked for. He said, "We (Paul and Barnabas) tell you the good news." True, Jesus did not deserve to die, true they killed him and nailed him to a tree, true they buried him in a borrowed grave, "But God" — (there's that wonderful phrase that we find over and over again in Acts) — "But God raised him from the dead!" The Christian faith and hope of the resurrection is a glorious one. It's a divine-shot-in-the-arm (or heart) for depression. The circumstances of life can only push us so far. The devil can only oppress us up to a certain point. We believe in the resurrection and nothing can ultimately defeat us!

On a tombstone, in a small, country churchyard, is carved just one word, "Forgiven," — no name, no indication of man or woman, no age or date, nothing more than "Forgiven." Much is missing from that marker, but what else really matters? Forgiveness is the essential need of us all. We cannot deny it. Deep down, in our heart of hearts, we are aware that we are terribly wrong, and we cannot "fix" it ourselves. We are not the wonderful people we have been told that we are, nor that we have told everyone we are. We are sinful. We have sinned against a holy God and are in need of a good word. What better word can there be for a person who is aware that he/she is a sinner — that through Christ there is forgiveness of sins! If this is not the message we are able to bring to a lost, sinful, dying humanity, then we have no message. This indispensable truth is for all who believe and accept Christ as Savior; whether they live in Nicaragua or North Carolina,

Mozambique or Minnesota, Palestine or Pennsylvania! There is forgiveness of sins for all who come to Christ through his cross.

Long ago Yugoslavia was ruled by kings of the Nemanyan dynasty, and all of them were crowned in the same great church in Zhitcha. When the time came for the coronation, a new door was cut in the wall for the new king to enter by, and when he went out afterward, the door was bricked up and never used again. But when Christ came from the grave, he too, opened a new door for us all. It was a door of forgiveness, a door to heaven, a door to eternal life. He made a new door, passed through it, and it was not bricked up afterward — it was left wide open for all who believe in him and follow in his new life of forgiveness.

Yes, the sure and depressing word is that we are sinners — all of us — but the "encouraging word" is that Christ died for sinners and there is for us, unworthy as we are, forgiveness of sins.

I daresay you feel better already!

Easter 5
Acts 14:8-18

Beware! Caution! Danger!

We may not always heed warning signs, but we still like to feel we have been told of approaching danger. We see signs everywhere that read: "Beware of the Dog," "Watch Your Step," "Danger! Thin Ice," "No Smoking. Oxygen in Use," "Watch for Wet Paint," "Dangerous Crossing," "Caution! No Lifeguard on Duty," and on and on they go. One cannot help but recall the story of the preacher who stood and announced his text. He began to read with increasing fervor, "Behold, I come quickly!" Then, for added emphasis, he read it again, "Behold, I come quickly!" Then he stepped to the edge of the chancel platform, and in a loud, commanding voice, repeated, "Behold, I come quickly!" Just then, he lost his balance, fell off the pulpit platform, and right into the lap of a lady seated in the front row. Terribly embarrassed, he began to apologize profusely. She interrupted the apology to say, "It's all right, pastor. After all, you warned me three times!"

This text is a warning. It is not one of the happier, positive sections of the Word, but it does have some high moments in it. And there is no doubt about the valuable lessons we can learn.

Beware The Temptation To Take Praise To Yourself

Paul and Barnabas are still on their first missionary journey, and now have moved to Lystra where they are involved in a strange incident. Paul healed a crippled man, and the people of Lystra are so impressed that they are determined to make gods of them.

It seems that there was a legendary history of Lyconia that told of Zeus and Hermes coming to earth incognito and in disguise. There was none in all the land who would grant hospitality to them, except for on old peasant couple who took them in and treated them kindly. The result was that the whole population of Lystra was wiped out by the gods, except for the old man and woman who took them in.

Now the people of Lystra are so carried away with the miracle of healing that they suspect that Barnabas, with his imposing appearance, is Zeus, the king of the gods, and Paul is Hermes, the god of speech, because he seems to be the main spokesman. Then, too, they don't want to get caught as they were before when they slammed their doors in the face of the gods. After all, you have to watch out for these gods. They get pretty touchy when they aren't treated right, and the people don't want to get in their bad graces again.

So it was that in most places, the people had heard Paul and Barnabas gladly, but these folks were too eager. They want to deify them. They heard little of what Paul and Barnabas had to say of salvation. They were so excited about a visit from the gods that they lost the message entirely. "The gods have come down to us in the likeness of men!" they shouted. Then they began to plan ways to celebrate the presence of the "gods" among them. Oxen were prepared for sacrifice, garlands of flowers were woven to honor them, and the festivities began to get bigger and wilder and more and more expansive. What a tumultuous welcome the apostles were receiving!

But when it dawned upon Paul and Barnabas what was happening, they were horrified. These people had not heard the gospel preached at all. Instead they were going to put the messengers in the Greek pantheon. They always had a lot of gods there and there was always room for one more (in this case, two more). Paul and Barnabas wondered what they could do. How could they proclaim the truth of the one, true, living God when these Lystrans were so mistaken? The apostles tore their garments — not a very godlike thing to do, when you think about it — but it was a radical Hebrew way of expressing horror and dismay over such a sacrilege. They had to help these men of Lystra realize that they were badly mistaken. They protested, "We, too, are only men, human like you." They wanted them to know they have the same kinds of problems all humans have; they bleed when they are cut, they suffer fatigue, they grow hungry, they are no different from anyone else.

Paul and Barnabas wanted no personal triumph for themselves, no crowning with garlands as gods, while their message was being ignored. So with strong words they turned the spotlight away from themselves and centered it upon the message they had brought.

Christian ministers, and Christian workers still have a similar danger in our time. Power, even power for good, is sometimes misinterpreted and misunderstood. Just as the dramatic healing drew a crowd at Lystra — or is seen on Sunday morning television — so it is dangerous when one is mistaken as the source of the power which belongs to God. Sometimes when I am conducting revival services I am asked to pray for the sick, and sometimes in marvelous grace and mercy, God will heal the individual. Then it is my responsibility to let it be clearly understood, "I am not the healer!" God heals them, when any divine grace is given, the work is always God's and his alone! Every misapprehension must be corrected when others would give the glory and praise to a human. Paul had it right when he said, "We preach not ourselves, but Christ crucified." All persons who work for Christ would do well to remember that "God is a jealous God and his glory he will not give to another."

This is not always easy to achieve; this shifting of attention away from one's self. A lot of the messenger's effectiveness, be it preacher, teacher, singer, worker, or whatever representative of the gospel, comes from his personal qualities. Marshall MacLuhen, mass media expert, said, "The medium is the message," and Phillips Brooks spoke of the same truth when he said, "truth through personality." When one deletes entirely the play of personal gifts, talents, and graces, it sometimes enfeebles the message. Of course all of this must be kept in a tension and balance with a strong God awareness that remembers that too much attention centered upon the messenger tends to dim and diminish the truth he is bringing.

Every preacher who takes his calling seriously, must make Christ preeminent in all things. There are always subtle temptations to take some of the praise to oneself. But this clever lure to self-aggrandizement is a danger to personal integrity. Caution must be given so that we never fail to give our undivided allegiance to Christ and Christ alone. John the Baptist had the proper motivation when he cried, "He must increase and I must decrease."

Motivation for Christian service has to be screened at all times. We must often ask ourselves, "Do I do this for Christ, or so that people will say, 'What a fine job you've done,' 'What would we ever do without you,' 'You are one of the best we've ever had!' " Helmut Thielicke, in his book, *Life Can Begin Again,* tells how he was once taken care of by a nurse who did her work perfectly. She told him that for 20 years she had worked on the night shift. Thielicke asked her if the strain were not tremendous, and where did she get her strength? She said, "Well, every night that I work puts another jewel in my crown, and I already have 7,175 in a row!" He said some of his gratitude for her immediately vanished, for he could no longer feel she was doing it out of concern for him, but instead had her eyes secretly fixed on that crown in heaven. Jesus reminded us that pure motivation in our good deeds is important. He said, "If your alms are given to be seen of men, you already have your reward."

It is so easy to fall into the trap of accepting the garlands of praise, and forget who we are serving. Paul took the only route that any of us can take. He disclaimed any kinship with the gods, and reminded those who would place him on a pedestal that he was "just like they were." Paul lived out that conviction of self-abasement in all his ministry. Later he would write, "It is no longer I that live, but Christ liveth in me."

Beware The Temptation To Compromise The Truth

The crowd at Lystra tried to blunt the edge of this new Christian truth by putting it in with the old categories. If they could just get these two new personalities, Paul and Barnabas, who had a new message, to conform to the old familiar gods, they would be safe. They would not need to change if they could just add on this new message to the old precepts and traditions.

This is a trick that has been around for a long time. The Greeks had a whole pantheon of gods; syncretism was nothing new. Why not just combine and reconcile all the gods and concepts and become tolerant of every other belief that came down the pike?

Doesn't that sound familiar? There are those who still try to press the gospel into molds that make it more palatable to all; new age, pluralism, humanism, and anything else that spares us from the radical allegiance that Christ calls us unto. The Christian gospel can easily be distorted beyond all recognition. How skillful we become in proclaiming tolerance, acceptance, and good in all other religions, until the unique truth of salvation through Christ is warped into a one-size-fits-all-religion.

I admit to frustration by the well-intentioned comments of those who so glibly say, "Well, after all, we're all headed for the same place," or "We all worship the same God, don't we?" I know they mean well, but how very dangerous such comments are! I believe in tolerance as much as is humanly possible, and will almost run from most fights, but when we must compromise the basic truth of the Bible, then we finally must recoil in horror, and say, "No, no, no!" One God is not as good as another, we do not all go to the same place, we do not all worship the same Lord. Christ is essential and imperative, and knowing him is the difference between eternal life and death! Other religions do have much to be respected and admired, but they do not offer equally salvific paths to God. A religion, as many are, that is diametrically opposed to Christianity cannot be right.

We live in a relational day when many are saying, "Relate to me, don't confront me." But where is the thundering spokesperson for God, saying "Repent, or ye shall all likewise perish?" Instead we are advised to use "soft terms," so rather than speaking of the absolutes of the Christian faith we speak of relevancies. But changing words does not change the facts. Sinners still need a Savior, and Christ died to save us from sin. Sin is a reality. The prophet said, "Woe to them that call evil good, and good evil; that put darkness for light, and light for darkness; that put bitter for sweet, and sweet for bitter (Isaiah 5:20)."

Just suppose Martin Luther had been asked (maybe at a potluck, ecumenical church supper with Germans and Italians), "Luther did you or did you not write these books?" Suppose Luther had replied, "Well, perhaps I have been a tad negative, but you know I've had problems with my self-esteem lately, and everyone has a bad day now and then." And they could have replied, "Okay, Martin, let's just take your books out of circulation and your theses off the door, and let's try to understand one another a little better. After all we worship the same God. We simply choose different ways of doing it."

Crazy, isn't it? But this scenario is no more foolish than replacing, "Ye must be born again," with "Let's all try a little harder to be tolerant, because God is such a God of love he would never let anyone be lost." When will we ever get it through our heads that Christ is the Way, and that we walk in darkness toward certain destruction without his grace and salvation? When we forsake the illumination of the Word and Christ the true Light, we become like blind men looking in a dark room for a black cat that isn't there.

The Lystra crowd was not opposed to another god or two, they just didn't want their old ones destroyed. David L. McKenna, President of Asbury Theological Seminary, was quoted in *International Christian Digest* as saying, "When we confess that Christ alone is the universal hope for our salvation, we indict all utopian schemes and humanistic programs in which the church gets embroiled."

Paul, who had been blinded on the Damascus Road, and then had both his physical eyes and the eyes of his soul enlightened, had caught a vision of Christ that remained clear and unshadowed by the temptation to take praise to himself or to compromise the truth of the gospel. May God grant that the same zealous fervor possess all those who follow in his train!

I was teaching a course on preaching some time ago at Salem College in Winston-Salem, North Carolina. The course was being offered in conjunction with the annual Moravian Music Festival, and the preachers taking the class were all Moravian ministers. One of the persons in attendance was The Right Reverend Jay Hughes, Bishop of the Moravian Church, who told of a time when he was pastor of the Home Moravian Church in Old Salem. There came into his study an old man; Brother Heath. He had been a stalwart giant of the Christian faith, a missionary who had translated the New Testament into several languages, and was now back in America. He was 80 years old. He said to the pastor, "Brother Hughes, you will probably conduct my funeral. I want you to promise me that when I die you will say very little of George Heath, and very much of Christ. Tell them of him!" Count Zinzendorf had the same conviction about it when he said, "I have one passion, it is he."

One More Warning: Not Everyone Will Like It!

But you need to be warned: people won't like it if you take their gods away. You see, it is far easier to make matinee idols (or television celebrities, or "jolly good fellows") out of our leaders than to hear the message. It is far easier to make new gods — and keep the old ones — than to accept the Gospel and come under the Lordship of Jesus Christ.

Notice how quickly the atmosphere changed when Paul and Barnabas, these "visiting gods," refused to be exalted and deified. The rest of the chapter, not a part of today's text, reads that Paul was stoned by the bitter, angry mob at Lystra. He was left on a garbage heap outside the city, for they believed he was dead. You see, folks become very threatened when a "new god" wants to take over their lives and replace the old habits and the old ways.

Happy endings are not always immediate for the Christian who will not compromise faith and convictions, but things do have a way of being all right. Paul was not dead, and once again Paul proclaims the message, and this time many believed! When he returned on his second missionary journey he found waiting for him a strong, vital church. When it is "Jesus first," and "Jesus only," you lose some and you win some — but you always win more than you lose!

Easter 6
Acts 15:1-2, 11, 22-29

Grace Is An "Inside Job!"

We live in a high-gloss, fix-the-outside, cover-up-the-spots world. We believe in making good first impressions, so we are very adept at cover-ups and shining up the outside. We have cover-ups in politics, in the world of high finance, in big business, and in education. Even if you buy peaches or strawberries from a road-side fruit stand you have to watch lest they have put the smaller, maybe rotten, fruit on the bottom, and then entice you to purchace them by covering it with the larger, more beautiful fruit on top.

So, it seems it had to happen sooner or later, the temptation to fix-up would arise in the new fledgling church that God was bringing into being. With the exception of the events at Lystra, and a few other setbacks, things have been going fairly well with Paul and Barnabas as they are going from place to place, preaching salvation through the crucified, risen, ascended Christ. But now, some men come along who want to take away from the simplicity of the gospel message. It all began over a discussion by some men in Jerusalem who had arrived in Antioch. They were insisting that the rite of circumcision was essential to Christian salvation. This would, of course, make the grace of God through faith in Jesus Christ, subject to the Mosaic law and make Christ himself subject to Moses. These Jews felt it was all right for the gentiles to become Christians, but first they must be circumcised; meaning that they first become Jews and then could be Christians.

So a conference was called, and the decision was reached that gentiles are equal in all religious matters to Jews, for both alike are dependent upon the grace of God in Jesus Christ for salvation. Therefore, circumcision was not required for salvation, because grace alone, assures us of salvation! Bishop William R. Cannon, in his commentary, *The Book of Acts,* says, "Next to the description of Pentecost in the second chapter of Acts, this passage is the most important in the entire book, for what takes place here opens up for the church its largest field for expansion and makes possible the eventual winning of the Roman Empire to Christianity." From this point on, Christianity is not just a part of a small Jewish sect, but it will become an independent movement, growing into the New Testament church.

Our text, then, gives us the formal letter that was drawn up, announcing that the mother church at Jerusalem had made this firm decision. Wisely, they decided to send, along with Paul and Barnabas, two other emissaries who were both prophets; Judas Barsabbas and Silas. Paul and Barnabas were already well-known in the early church, beloved because they had often risked their lives for Jesus Christ. The letter went on to mention some reasonable restrictions for the new gentile Christians, but these limitations would be helpful to Jew and gentile alike, in that they would aid the new Christians in avoiding participation in pagan worship in any form.

We have here, then, some vital and important lessons for those early Christians, but also for all of us who follow in their train:

Grace Is Not What You Do

This entire chapter deals with what was then, and continues to be, a stumbling block for the Christian gospel. There are always those persons, however well-meaning they may be, who would make salvation possible through Jesus Christ, plus something else! But salvation is through grace and grace alone, and anything added to that is heresy!

It is understandable how this came about. These Jewish Christians had, for centuries, known a religion based on laws, precepts, rules, and regulations. But now they are told it was a work done in the heart; an "inside job," not an external act. This inner work is accomplished by the Holy Spirit, and not the work of circumcision, or any other good work, which brings redemption.

But it is hard to break old habits. Paul had to deal with this again and again. Romans and Galatians speak to the problem repeatedly. He had to keep preaching that Christian freedom is in Christ, and converts must not be encumbered again with the slavery of works righteousness. "For in Christ Jesus, neither circumcision nor uncircumcision has any value. The only thing that counts is faith expressing itself through love (Galatians 5:6)."

The Roman Catholic Church burdened its constituents with rules, regulations, and the purchasing of indulgences to "buy" favor with God. The Reformation was a frontal assault against externals being able to pacify God; but rather the glorious liberating truth of grace alone. Now here we are, nearing the 21st century, and often find ourselves still trying to "do" something to be saved. We work so hard at being "good enough" and hope that the balance sheet shows we are on the "good side of God." It is so difficult to move from the Old Covenant to the New Covenant, from the outer rule to inner experience, from doctrines to life, from rules to revelation, from law to grace.

For many years I felt that God would love and accept me only if I could be "good enough" to please him. I was constantly trying to "shape up," to "do better," to "try harder." How miserable I was, and what a nervous Christian I became. I figured that God had a record book that he kept in heaven. On the page with my name at the top he had drawn a line down the center, with debits and credits on either side of the center. On a good day I might tally enough "plus points" to be pleasing and acceptable to God; while on a bad day I would be afraid to go to sleep at night lest I had not "earned" the right to heaven if I should die before morning. It was the greatest freedom in the world to be delivered from that kind of works righteousness! When I realized that I was justified and forgiven; not because of obedience to the law, not because of rituals or holy habits, but because of a divine grace that never failed, I was emancipated and felt a marvelous deliverance. We are forgiven, absolutely and completely, when we repent of our sins and trust God's action in our behalf in Christ. Forgiveness cannot be earned nor merited, it has already been given, it can only be accepted by faith.

Bishop Taylor Smith, an evangelical stalwart, was one day sitting in a barber shop having a shave. When the bishop spoke of being made right with God, the barber replied, "I do my best and that's good enough for me." When the bishop's shave was finished, the next man took his place, and the bishop said, "May I shave this customer?" "Oh, no," replied the barber firmly. "But I would do my best," protested the bishop. "So you might," replied the barber, "but your best would not be good enough for this customer." "No, and neither is your best good enough for God," was the reply of Bishop Smith. Christianity is more than doing one's best, of "helping him out." It is letting God do his best for you, and that took place at the cross.

We keep working on externals, but God wants to work on the internal. We try to whitewash ourselves, but only God can wash us white!

Grace Is What Christ Has Done

Salvation is not what we can do, but what Christ has done. God purifies the heart by faith, so why put on a yoke of circumcision, or any other external requirement?

We are saved through grace. When God looks at us, he doesn't see us, he sees Christ. We "wear" him. We are covered by his blood, hidden in him, covered with his robe of righteousness. He doesn't even remember our sins. He forgets them. He blots out the record against us. He erases the writing of our offenses. He cleans the tape of evidence. He clears the computer. The horrible guilt of the past is covered with blood too precious to ever have been spilled in vain for us.

The St. Petersburg Times (November 1989) carried the report of a 21-month-old child who was dying. The baby's mother, Teresa Smith, risked her own life to give a part of her liver to her baby. Never before was there an operation taking a part of one person's liver and giving it to another. Someone commented on the extent of her love, but the mother said, a short while after the operation, "Once you've given someone a piece of your heart, it's easy to throw in a little bit of liver!" So with our Lord, once you've died on a cross, revealing a heart as big as the world, and loving enough to break and die for the sinner, it's a simple matter to accept the wondrous truth of his willingness to receive us. It would be rather presumptuous, don't you think, that a "wee bit of pain and flesh of circumcision" would need to be added?

We call this justification by grace through faith the process of being born again. What a tremendous experience is this new birth! We are sealed in the waters of Christian baptism and become new creatures in Christ Jesus.

Dr. Christian Bernard tells of one of his heart-transplant patients who asked to see his old heart which had been removed. Obligingly the doctor brought from the laboratory a large bottle where the old organ had been placed. As the man looked at the big muscle which once pumped life through his body, the famed surgeon suddenly realized that this was the first time in human history that a person had ever seen his own heart. It was a historic moment, but for the patient it must have been a keenly sensitive sensation, for the old heart had worn out and failed him. Now the old heart had been replaced by a new one, and without it his life would now be extinct. After gazing for a long moment at the old heart, the grateful patient looked up at the doctor and said, "I'm glad that I don't have that old heart anymore." This is the new life that Christ imparts to every person who is justified by faith and experiences the new birth. All of us desperately need a conversion that shatters the old life and makes all things new! That is why it is imperative that we know it is always an inside job. Cosmetic surgery will never do. We need a radical heart transplant.

The story is told of a plane that was bucking all over the sky as it hit some turbulence. A stewardess came to where Mohammed Ali sat, and said to him, "Mr. Ali, don't you think you should buckle your seat belt? This flight is becoming very rough." Ali replied, "Honey, Superman don't need no belt!" The flight attendant retorted, "Honey, Superman don't need no plane!" The self-righteous don't need a Savior. Those who think they can fix themselves don't need Christ.

William Temple once said, "It is no good giving me a play like *Hamlet*, or *King Lear,* and telling me to write a play like that. Shakespeare could do it; I can't. And it is no good showing me a life like the life of Jesus, and telling me to live a life like that. Jesus could do it; I can't. But, if the genius of Shakespeare could come and live in me, then I could write plays like that. And if the Spirit of Jesus could come and live in me, then I could live a life like that." This is the only way the Christian can be holy and good. It is not circumcision, or anything else we do, it is always what he does in us!

Now Do As He Commands

But what about "works." Are we not to do some good deeds? Yes, these early Christians were given some restrictions and ordinances that were to be kept. They were not to be kept in order to become Christians, but because they were Christians they would keep them. Out of a heart of gratitude and love for all that Christ has done for us, we naturally do good works. When we live in the Spirit, the natural outgrowth is good works. The letter of the law required holiness, but the Spirit imparts holiness. Jesus did not come to teach a new philosophy, but to bring a new life. He did not come with a new rule, but a new Spirit and a new attitude. The Old Covenant is letter, the New Covenant is Spirit.

The law was an external matter, grace is an internal matter and it works by faith. Christ is now with you all the time. You are in a relationship with him, the closest relationship a person can possibly have. Christ is inside you! Did you ever notice that Paul had Christ in him whether he was in the pulpit or in jail? So do we, and when Christ is in us, the good works are a natural fruit and evidence of his presence.

So now we see a difference between faith and works. Works are not for salvation. Salvation comes through the work of Christ at Calvary, and him alone. We respond to his call in repentance and faith, and we are justified by grace through faith. Our sanctification, then, is the living out of that faith in good works. Good works do not make you a Christian, they identify you as a Christian. Love for Christ is what makes us want to keep his commandments, makes us desire to never sin again, makes us want to be different, makes us want to give our Lord our best. The prayer of the hymn becomes our own, "More love to Thee, O Christ, more love to Thee!"

Ascension Sunday
Acts 1:1-11

The "Ups And Downs" Of The Ascension

Roller coasters are becoming more and more popular in America; they are being built taller, and longer, and faster — and nearly every major theme and play park seems to have one. In a world that keeps us as dizzy as being on a roller coaster, or at best we have a suspicion that we are being used as a yo-yo, trying to meet the demands of all the strident voices about us. So, when a church event that has its anniversary on a certain Thursday every year — not even a Sunday — we find it a bit difficult to get too excited about the Ascension of our Lord. But lest we miss its true importance, let us look at it one more time. Jesus and his little band of followers are standing on a knoll called Mount Olivet, within sight of Jerusalem, and emotions are running high. Jesus is about to leave them — again! Some few days ago he told them he had to die, and he did — on another hill called Calvary, also within sight of Jerusalem. That first time he was taken away from them by force, then lifted up on a cross to die an agonizing death in redeeming a sinful world back to God. But God raised him up, and now he has been with them again for 40 days. They have felt once more his loving, familiar, comforting presence, and so his announcement of another departure — this time a permanent one — is not easy to accept. This time he will not be lifted "up" on a cross, but will go "up" to the Father in heaven. He said that it was "expedient for them, so that the Comforter could come, the Spirit who would abide with them forever." As they watch, a cloud receives him out of their sight as their Lord ascends to his Father in heaven. The reassuring words of the two men in white garments (were they not likely angels?) must have helped a bit when they were told,

"This same Jesus will come again, just as you have seen him go into heaven." But when will he come again? and how? and what about the days in-between his leaving them and his return? what does it all mean? For that matter, what does a lesson like this mean to you and me?

Let us remind ourselves not to be so concerned with the literalism of the events of the text that we lose sight of the glorious message. When you start worrying about the accuracies of the account that comes to us from a pre-scientific world, you run into all sorts of problems. Just saying that Jesus went "up" boggles our minds; "up" from where, to where? The three-story universe understanding of the biblical writers (a flat earth with heaven above and hades beneath) causes all sorts of questions and speculations about the Ascension. After all, in our world we send astronauts up, but stock markets go down; prices go up, and profits go down; unemployment goes up, and ratings go down; cost of living goes up, grades go down. Now those "ups and downs" we readily understand!

But what is this all about: Jesus went "up" and the Spirit will come "down?" Does it have any practical application for those of us who live realistically in a world that constantly teeters on the brink of disaster? Since we all long for certitude and stability, why does the church feel this doctrine of the Ascension of our Lord is so important?

Note that the early church was not overly concerned about the scientific and factual details of this event. Rather, they embraced the Ascension as an eternal truth that served to steady their faith, universalize the gospel and energize their witness. Look at these splendid truths:

The Ascension Announces A Throne

"So then after the Lord had spoken to them, he was received up into heaven, and sat on the right hand of God (Mark 16:19-20)." The Christ who once walked among us, died on a cross for us, rose from the dead, now lives and reigns!

What a glorious truth! Jesus now reigns in heaven! Jesus is on the throne. In the chapel of Edward the Confessor, in Westminster Abbey in London, is the Coronation chair. It has been in use since 1301. All the reigning monarchs of England have sat upon it for their coronation. It is marked, marred, scratched, and rather ugly. Initials and names are carved on it like so much graffiti. It may not be beautiful, but it is a national treasure in Great Britain. I wonder what Christ's coronation chair is like in heaven? Imagine! Provided by the Father so that he can rule at his right hand! Perhaps it has "King of kings" and "Lord of lords" inscribed on its back. Maybe it is set with the very diadems of heaven — but no matter what it looks like, its glory is dimmed by the brightness of the One who sits upon it.

Christ is there as our Savior and Redeemer. The marks of our redemption are upon him, and we shall know him by his nail-pierced hands. And he also reigns as our high priest, intercessor, and advocate. We lift our prayers to God the Father, but close them "in Jesus' name," or "for Jesus' sake." But he is there, too, as Lord and King. Right now, he rules over human affairs and destinies from his throne in heaven. The new hymnal of the United Methodist Church has a chorus which says, "Majesty, worship His majesty. Unto Jesus be all glory, honor, and praise. Majesty, kingdom authority flow from His throne unto His own: His anthem raise. So exalt, lift up on high the name of Jesus. Magnify, come glorify Christ Jesus the King. Majesty, worship His majesty; Jesus who died, now glorified, King of all kings."

Perhaps that song writer had been reading Paul's words: "Therefore God exalted him to the highest place and gave him the name that is above every name, that at the name of Jesus every knee should bow, in heaven and on earth and under the earth, and every tongue confess that Jesus Christ is Lord, to the glory of God the Father (Philippians 2:9-11)."

Did you really think that his absence from earth meant that our affairs and problems are out of his mind? out of his hands? The Sovereign Son is still absolutely in charge! The church is not limited to our puny, earthbound resources because Jesus of Nazareth, son of a peasant woman and a carpenter, Jesus the teacher, Christ the crucified Savior, has now gone "up" to share in God's rule over heaven and earth. He sits at the Father's own right hand.

When Christ was on earth he was local and limited to time and space. His followers saw his visible form, but he could not belong to the whole world. Only by departing from the sight of the privileged few could he reign, by his Spirit, in the hearts of all. Christ is no longer localized in that tiny spot of earth we call the Holy Land. He has gone above to rule, to put all things under his feet.

The doctrine of the ascension gives us faith for these last days, and for our darkest days. It is important to remember "who" rules in the affairs of the human condition. Those first disciples feared he was leaving, but he told them he was not going "away," but "up." And there is a big difference!

Dr. Robert Stackel quotes someone as saying that with the passing away from the rule of so many kings in our world, the prophecy has been made that by the year 2000, there will be only five kings left: The King/Queen of England, and the king of spades, hearts, diamonds, and clubs. No matter: the Christian has a mighty King that will never be de-throned, and he shall reign forever and ever! All that mankind has done, or can do, is under the sovereignty of Jesus Christ. Nothing can override or overrule him. He is in charge!

The Ascension Announces A Testimony

The disciples were promised that when Jesus went "up" the Spirit would come "down," and "ye shall be my witnesses (Acts 1:8)."

When Luke gives his other description of the ascension, in the gospel bearing his name, he says that after Christ was taken "up," "they went forth and preached everywhere." Christ sat down on the throne and the Christians went forth to witness, to preach, and to bear testimony. Christ was at the Father's right hand in heaven and the disciples were busy evangelizing. Christ took his departure from them and they were convinced that now they were his agents on earth to carry out the work he had begun. Jesus had said to Peter, James, and John, "As the Father hath sent me, even so send I you."

Christ is now enthroned in the place of power and authority, and the disciples are now energized by the coming of the Holy Spirit, and they set out to bear their witness to Christ, and that testimony will evangelize a hostile world. They are accused of "turning the world upside down," but in truth they were turning it "right side up."

Disciples are still bearing the testimony to Christ, and it is making a difference in the world. *Christianity Today* reported that the world's Christian population grew by about 326 million during the 1980s, and Christians now number an estimated 1.75 billion. The total amounts to about 33 percent of the world's 5.3 billion people. But we cannot lie back on our laurels, for America remains one of the greatest of all mission fields for the gospel. We total some 242 million persons, and, according to *Pulpit Helps* (July 1990) 167 million Americans do not know Christ as Savior and Lord. The number of the unconverted in America increases by about 2 million each year.

We are sorely in need of impassioned hearts and dedicated tongues to bear witness to the Christ. Psychologists estimate that the average person is each day given 700 chances to say something. Talkative people utter about 12,000 sentences each day, which averages out to a little over 100,000 words. Would it not seem that at least some of those words should be spoken for the Savior? Perhaps we all live somewhere between the stammer of our speaking and the grace of God. It ought not to be difficult to speak of him, if he has claimed our hearts and won our love. Strange, isn't it; we can talk about sex, or sports (sometimes it's almost pathological, our rabid interest in sports), or children, or grandchildren — why then, can we not talk about our Lord? God wants us to name his name in conversations (and not as a swear-word). We may stammer, we may stutter, we may blush, but for Jesus' sake, let us dare speak!

Of course, often our attitude and our spirit is just as important as words. I claim a dear, young couple as friends. Awhile back they told me of an incident in their lives. Jon is the editor and owner of one of the county newspapers. He'd been working hard all week, and wanted to go golfing. Lynn, his wife, wanted him to work in the yard. Jon said, "But I've only played golf once all year. I'll work in the yard later." Lynn replied, "Go on then and play golf, I don't care what you do!" Jon came home some hours later, relaxed and happy with his golf game; but Lynn was far from feeling the same way. She was quiet, mad, and the atmosphere fairly pulsated with her displeasure. This went on for two or three days, and the air was still heavy with unspoken feelings. Finally, when Jon saw things were not getting any better, he said, "Lynn, let's talk about this. I don't understand. What's wrong? You told me you didn't care what I did." Lynn blurted out, "Jon, I can't believe that you believed what I told you!" No, our Christian witness is not all words about Jesus, it is sometimes a spirit and an attitude that convinces others of his reality in our lives.

A missionary doctor in an overseas hospital removed cataracts from a man's eyes and restored his sight. A few weeks later, the doctor was surprised to see 48 men blind men coming towards the hospital. Each one held onto a rope which was guided by the man who had recently gotten his sight back. He had led them on the rope a distance of 250 miles from one of the interior provinces to the doctor who was able to help nearly all of them receive his sight.

We have a story to tell, a testimony to give, a witness to make about the one who has opened our sin-blinded eyes to the light of the gospel. Since Christ's coronation we all have a great commission: "All authority has been given me in heaven and on earth, now go ye into all the world and preach the gospel to every creature." We are commissioned as Christ's ambassadors, we are his heralds. By our life and lips we are witnesses of the reigning Lord. Our cause must not, will not, cannot fail!

The Ascension Announces A Triumph

"This same Jesus . . . will come back (Acts 1:11)." So the ascension of Christ did not mean his permanent absence after all! As surely as Christ now sits enthroned, as surely as we are called to testify to our faith by the empowering Spirit, just that sure is the fact of Christ's returning. When? Who knows? It could happen at any time, at any moment. It could be just around the corner, or it might be a lot longer. But let us not be side-tracked with idle speculations as to dates, but consider instead what its actuality will mean to us.

On December 17, 1903, Orville and Wilbur Wright were able to keep their hand-built airplane in the air for 59 seconds. This was a moment that changed history. In their excitement, they immediately sent a telegram to their sister back in Dayton, Ohio. It read: "Sustained flight today for 59 seconds. Hope to be home by Christmas." Their sister was so excited by the staggering good news that she took the telegram with its big, history-making words, to the editor of the local newspaper. The next morning, to her surprise, the sister read the bold headlines splashed across the newspaper: "Popular local bicycle merchants to be home for the holidays!" We, too, dare not miss the point of our Lord's return. The "when" is trivia, the "fact" is vital!

In *Fiddler on the Roof,* a young man asks his rabbi, "Wouldn't this be a good time for the Messiah to come?" It would — it would indeed. The time is ripe for the second coming of Christ.

The return of Christ is not a threat, but a fulfillment of a glorious and wonderful promise to the Christian: "This same Jesus . . . will come back!"

At Christ's coming there will finally be peace on earth. Imagine it! On this poor, war-ravaged earth peace has never been known. It seems that somewhere on this beleagured planet that there is always a nation or people at war, but when Christ returns, war will be no more. Swords will be made into plowshares, and spears into pruning hooks.

Christ's return will mean that justice will finally be done. The creeds say, "Christ shall come to judge the living and the dead." Justice demands that there be a reckoning day when wrongs are made right. On earth, justice is not always done. How many times have we looked at a situation and cried, "It's simply not fair!" Super criminals die without paying in this life for their evil deeds. Murderers are released after three or seven years in prison. Think of Hitler, Stalin, Khomeni, and others who were responsible for the deaths of millions. When Christ returns, justice will be meted out.

Simple reason asks for a meaning to history. The world does not go on and on without purpose. Is this world simply to be kept running until it runs out of steam, or until the sun cools, or until nuclear war destroys it, or until the ice age appears, or some other threatening calamity causes a global annhilation? In whose hands is the fate of the earth: human hands or God's hands? Does he really have "the whole world in his hands?" Yes, he does! We believe that history is linear, not circular. We Christians believe that history is "his story." God is in charge; always has been, always will be. This is "our Father's world," not the devil's world, not the world of evil men and women. When Christ appears, history will come to a meaningful end with full victory for truth and righteousness.

So we labor at the task of testifying to God's grace, believing that a "This same Jesus . . . will come back." There is a story of tourist that some years ago visited a castle along Lake Como in Italy. A friendly old gardener opened the gates and showed him the gardens. He asked the old man, "When was your master last here?" He replied, "Twelve years ago." "Does he never come by to see how things are going?" the tourist asked. "Never," replied the gardener. The tourist exclaimed, "But you keep the garden in such fine condition. It is as though you expected your master to come tomorrow." Promptly the old man replied, "No, today, sir, today." The Savior we call Lord could come tomorrow, or next year, or today — it doesn't really matter as long as we are ready for his appearing. He walked among us as the Lamb of God that takes away the sins of the world, but his next return will reveal him as the conquering Lion of Judah as he comes in majesty and glory.

Charles Wesley had this glorious triumph in mind when he wrote:

> *Lo, he comes with clouds descending,*
> *Once for favored sinners slain,*
> *Thousand, thousand saints attending*
> *Swell the triumph of his train:*
> *Hallelujah! Hallelujah! Hallelujah!*
> *God appears on earth to reign,*
> *God appears on earth to reign!*

Christians Have More "Ups Than Downs"

Christ came "down" at Christmas, he was lifted "up" upon a cross, he was buried, a real "downer" — but God raised him "up" from the dead, he ascended "up" to the Father, The Holy Spirit came "down" to empower the church, Christ will come "down" again, and take us "up" to heaven to ever dwell with him. Yes, the Christian life has its "ups and downs," but always it looks "up," knowing that redemption draweth nigh! "Up" is the language of the ascension, and of God, and the hope of us all!

Pentecost
Genesis 11:1-9
Acts 2:1-12

Death Of A Dream — Birth Of A Church

This Old Testament lesson is a story of failure, but there is a great truth for all of us in it. I had a dear friend who used to say, "Every man is my teacher. I either learn what to do from him, or what not to do." It reminds me of a cartoon, which showed a bum sitting on a park bench; his clothes were tattered and torn, his toes were coming out of his shoes — the stereotypical hobo. Beneath the picture was the caption, "No man is completely worthless — he can always serve as a horrible example." And so from this Genesis text we learn from it what to avoid doing rather than what to do.

The church, in choosing lections for each Sunday, oddly enough has linked this text with the second chapter of Acts, which gives the account of the descent of the Holy Spirit. The Tower of Babel in Genesis has little, or nothing, to do with the Day of Pentecost, and yet when you examine these widely divergent passages, there are some amazing comparisons and sharp contrasts between them.

Let us keep foremost before us the realization that the Day of Pentecost is one of the three great days of the Christian year. Only Christmas and Easter precede it in importance, and since Christmas rarely falls on a Sunday, Pentecost is second only to Easter as the most important Sunday of the Christian year.

Let us look at these accounts, separately, and find how they speak to us:

The Death Of A Dream — The Tower Of Babel

When the Peachtree Plaza Hotel was built in Atlanta a few years ago it was the tallest hotel in the world. It dominated the city skyline, a towering steel, silo-like building that was the focal point for the entire area. Likewise, if you had been in the area of Shinar, and had looked out across the plain, you would have seen a strikingly tall structure — in truth it was the world's first skyscraper. But this tower was never completed. It appeared to be well-built, up to a point, but as your eyes followed to its apex you see that it is still unfinished.

Pride

Hal Roach, Ireland's famous international comedian, tells the story of the two Irishmen, Casey and Flanagan, who were building a 500-foot tower. Just as they were putting the final brick in place, Casey happened to glance at the blueprints. He said to Flanagan, "We're stupid fools, the two of us. We've been reading the plans of the tower upside down. We are supposed to be digging a well!" The men of Shinar did not have their blueprints upside down. They intended to build a tower. But, if you were looking at it, you might wonder why it was never finished. Even more importantly, you might ask, "Why was it built in the first place? A lot of possibilities might occur to you: Did these people want a prayer tower? Did they want this structure to bring them closer to God? Was it to be a haven in which to hide from their enemies? Could it have been a hotel for the homeless? Was it meant as a hospital for the sick? If you thought any of these were the reasons, you would have been wrong. The tower was built for self-aggrandizement. They said, "Let us build a tower that reaches to the heavens, so that we can make a name for ourselves." It was not a monument to the glory of God, it was a shrine to themselves. They were ambitious for the pride and the glory of their own names.

They did have one thing in their favor. They had a strong chance of their project being a success, because they were united. They had one mind: "Let us make a name for ourselves." You can accomplish a lot if there is unity in the plan. In the horse-and-buggy days, a boy was driving along a road with a farmer who was very skilled in the finer flickings of the whip. When a fly setled on the horse's back, a swift flick of the lash would remove it without disturbing the horse. If he saw a bee on a roadside flower, it would swiftly disappear with the practiced accuracy of the whip aimed at it. Then the buggy passed near a tree from which hung a wasps' nest, but the driver held his whip quietly. "Why didn't you use your whip on those wasps?" asked the boy. "Well," the expert answered, "I thought I'd leave them alone. You see, they're organized." Even with such a poor reason for building a tower, the men were likely to succeed because they were organized with a common goal in mind.

Obviously, there is nothing wrong of itself in building a tall tower. It was the misdirection of the motivation that caused God's disfavor. We are not a lot different from the men of that day. We still think of self first, we look out for number one, and often ask, "What's in it for me?" When personalized license plates were introduced in Illinois, the Department of Motor Vehicles received over 1,000 requests for number 1. The state official whose job it was to approve the requests said, "I'm not going to assign it to someone and disappoint 1,000 other people, so I'll give it to myself!" Doesn't that make you think of the little boy and girl who were riding a mechanical horse in the shopping mall? The little boy, who was riding in front, turned to the little girl and said, "If one of us would get off, there would be more room for me!" We keep looking for ways to be number one: first in line, first at the check-out counter, first out of the crowded parking lot, first at the cafeteria on Sunday (ahead of the Baptists, Methodists, or whomever). The men of the Towel of Babel had no eye on God at all, just a good eye on self — and pride of self was a wrong reason. It always is.

Confusion

As good and loving and gracious as God is, we must never forget that "God is a jealous God, and his glory he will not give to another." With heavy disapproval upon these self-serving men in Babylon, he said, "Let us go down and confuse their language so they will not understand each other." And he did just that. He confused their language, and communication became impossible; therefore the finishing of the tower was a hopeless endeavor.

A man was in consultation with his physician, and complained of an unsatisfactory physical relationship with his wife. The doctor, an avid jogger, said, "What you need is some vigorous exercise. I want you to run 10 miles a day for 30 days, and then give me a call." True to the plan, the patient called his doctor at the end of the month. "How are you doing?" asked the doctor. "Has your relationship with your wife improved?" "How should I know?" exclaimed the patient, "I'm 300 miles from home!" A common language and communication is vital for success in any endeavor — but even if you have a unity in purpose and a common speech that is still not sufficient to supply attainment.

The late E. Stanley Jones said that "Human nature is allergic to sin and evil. You do as you like, and then you don't like what you do. You have your own way, and then you don't like your way. You express yourself, and you don't like the self you express." God will not long let us harbor our distorted values. Humans, left to go unchecked by the God to whom we are all accountable, will never, on their own, break away from the addiction of power and prestige and profit. It seems that no matter how much you achieve it is never enough. Dr. Leonard Sweet, in his book, *The Power of the Spirit,* said, "The dominant concept of power today revolves around money, muscle, multitudes, and might." Those unholy and unhealthy ambitions become a cancer in the soul, that eats away at the vitality that is good and pure and true and holy.

Failure

Evil may seem to prosper for a time, but when God intervenes, it is with a strong, sure stroke that brooks no argument.

There, on the plain of Shinar, God moved in and confused the language. When you can't communicate you are doomed to failure. And they did fail. There was a scattering of the people, and that was the end of the tower project.

Notice that there is always a strong centrifugal power in a godless spirit. Such a spirit has no strong center — remember, the center for them was the self — so it scatters, divides, and weakens the whole. There on Babylon's plain stands the unfinished Tower of Babel, where the people, under the punishment of God, went away babbling in all directions. There would not be a restoration of genuine speech for the human race until the Holy Spirit was given.

Let us look at that event in our text in Acts:

The Birth Of The Church — The Upper Room

Now we change locations. We move from the plain to the city, from Babylon to Jerusalem, from the Tower of Babel to the upper room.

Waiting

As you enter the upper room you notice an immediate difference. These folks are not busy building, but just waiting. They are waiting and praying. They, like the Babylonian tower builders, are united in their purpose. They, too, are of one mind, in one accord, with one common goal. But they don't seem to be actively engaged in a project. From all observation they haven't even appointed a committee to work on the problem yet. But, in the room you sense a keen expectancy. If one thought they ought to be "doing" something, one might well ask, "Don't you have any place else to go?" "Peter, couldn't you at least go back to fishing for awhile?" "Matthew, couldn't you return to collecting taxes?" Or, "Have you thought that you could build a great memorial there on

Mount Olivet, marking the exact spot where Jesus stood when he left to go to the Father?" "Have any of you thought of starting your own religion? Surely you've learned a lot from your former leader, so maybe now you could choose someone more acceptable to the majority of the populace."

But these suggestions would only fall on deaf ears. These disciples are obedient still to a Commander who has been promoted "upstairs." He said to wait, watch, tarry, and pray until the Holy Spirit came. He had promised the Spirit was the Comforter, and they could certainly use some of that, for their hearts are still hurting with the absence of the best friend they ever had!

But, if we continue to delve into the reasons for their presence here in the upper room, we might query, "How long will you have to wait?" Their reply, "He didn't say." "But," we persist, "how long have you been here now?" "Ten days," they respond. "Ten days! My goodness! How much longer are you going to hang on to that ethereal promise of an absent Lord with nothing to show for it?" Their reply, based on solid faith, "As long as it takes!" We might have gone away muttering, "They are crazy! They have lost their minds! Waiting for the Spirit, indeed. This is a real world we live in. They seemed so sane, but waiting for the Spirit is dementia." And so we'd have left them, and gone back to our safe, dry, listless, spiritless living in our "real world."

But waiting often is the very thing that is needed. Robert Schuller tells of a winter at home, when his dad needed firewood. He found a dead tree and sawed it down. In the spring, to his dismay, he found new shoots had sprouted from the trunk. He said to his son, "I thought sure it was dead; the leaves had dropped, the twigs snapped, it seemed as if there was no life there. But now I see there is still life at the taproot of the old tree." He looked at his boy and said, "Bob, don't forget this important lesson. Never cut down a tree in the wintertime. Never make a negative decision in a low time. Never make your most important decisions when you are in your worst mood. Wait. Be patient. The spring will come."

And so, the disciples waited 24 hours, then another day, then a week, and now it has been 10 days, but still they waited — waited and prayed!

I love the account of the old, dedicated preacher who got carried away with his subject one very cloudy, thunderous, lightning-flashing Sunday. He was preaching from the Old Testament about the power of God, and really got carried away with his message. The old pastor was so enthralled with his sermon that he had not noticed that the storm outside was increasing with fury. It finally got his attention when a window pane crashed inward, a tree limb fell against the building, and the wind began tearing shingles off the roof. The old church squeaked, creaked, and groaned in the storm, and a parishioner in the service yelled, "Pastor, quit your preachin' and start prayin' afore we all get blowed to kingdom come!" Finally, the old pastor, now filled with fear himself, changed gears and started to pray. But he hadn't had time to think about his prayer, so he went back to his text and prayed, "O Lord, send Moses to lead us out of this stormy wilderness. O God, send Abraham, Isaac, and Jacob to us. O Lord, send the children of Israel!" Another brother in the back of the church began to pray after the preacher, "O Lord, don't send any of them fellers, and 'specially don't send the children. This ain't no time for kids. O Lord, come yourself!" That's exactly what the upper room people were praying for; for God the Holy Spirit to come himself! They, like the tower builders, were united in a single purpose, but while the folks at Babel had the self in mind, the upper room disciples had only God in mind. Another big difference!

Wind

And suddenly — God often works that way, you know — suddenly there is the sound of a mighty rushing wind, and it fills all the place where they are sitting. It is no longer a quiet, uneventful, nothing-is-happening place; the upper room has become a Tower of Power!

The refreshing wind of the Spirit is blowing and it is changing the men and women who waited. It is causing things to begin to happen. The Holy Spirit's presence is always equated with power. Look at how this "wind of God" is described by the translators: Weymouth calls it "a blast," Moffatt says, "a violent blast," the NIV describes it as "a violent wind," and the NRSV says, "the rush of a violent wind." Others say similarly, "a terrific blast of wind," "a strong driving wind," "a strong wind," or "a mighty wind storm." Luccock reminds us that no one called it a "zephyr," a light gentle, breeze. Pentecost did not begin with a zephyr! The Spirit came with power and violence; not a destructive violence, but a strength that enabled great accomplishments.

As the violent wind shook the room, the disciples knew that something glorious was happening. They were immediately convinced that what they had been waiting for had begun. Christ had kept his promise to them! They would never doubt that their Lord had come to them in this unmistakeable way. The mighty breath of God (the Hebrew word for breath is *ruach*) was moving among them. Breath is life! We breathe 18 times a minute, 1,080 times an hour, 25,000 times a day. At age 40 you will have had 365 million breaths, each a gift from God, the gift of life. A few moments without breath and you are unconscious, a few moments more and you are dead. No wonder the psalmist declares, "Let everything that hath breath praise the Lord (Psalm 150:6)." On his death bed, John Wesley's last words were, "I'll praise . . . I'll praise . . ." He was struggling to say the words of the great hymn of Isaac Watts, "I'll Praise my Maker while I've Breath." What natural breath is to the human body for its existence, so is the mighty Breath of God (the Holy Spirit) to the spirit of a person. We simply cannot live long without him. We are more right than we knew when we pray as we sing, "Breathe on me Breath of God, Fill Me with Life Anew."

Witness

Then the visible sign appeared: "Tongues that seemed like fire touched each person there." Had Jesus not said that they would be baptized with the Holy Spirit and with fire? "And they were all filled with the Holy Spirit, and began to talk in other languages, as the Spirit enabled them to speak." Here, as at the Tower of Babel, we deal with language. But this time it is not the "confusion of the language," it is the use of many languages for communication with those who are present — languages used, ultimately, for conversion to Christ. Again, such a difference between Babel and Pentecost!

A Wycliffe missionary translator said that there are 6,000 languages in the world today, but that 3,500 languages yet are only oral and have to be put into written language and the Bible translated into them. We who use the English language sometimes forget that knowledge of other languages is imperative for the spread of the gospel. Bill Bryson, in his book, *The Mother Tongue: English and How it Got That Way,* says that English has become the language to know. It is spoken by a third of the world's population. Two-thirds of all scientific papers, half of all European business deals, and 70 percent of all the mail in the world are written in English. But the language native to the disciples on the Day of Pentecost was not English, but Aramaic. Luke is careful to say that all the visitors that were in Jerusalem on the Day of Pentecost — the Jews of Dispersion — spoke many languages. These people had come from all parts of the known world for the Feast of the Passover. And they heard the disciples speak in their own native tongue. They were from Parthia, Media, Elam, Mesopotamia, Judea, Cappadocia, Pontus, Asia, Phrygia, Pamphylia, Egypt, Crete, Arabia, Rome — and so the list goes on. Imagine their amazement! They all heard about the mighty acts of God in their own tongue. There can be no doubt that God intends everyone to know of the international character of Christianity, that the gospel is for the whole world, and that Christ is a universal Savior!

You can count on it: when the Holy Spirit is present, he makes Christ known to the hearts of those who will hear. I preached at a camp meeting a few years past. There was a local church nearby whose pastor had warned his people to stay away. He believed neither in camp meetings nor in women preachers, and did not want his people to attend. But one man came to each of the services. He felt the presence of the Spirit as God blessed with large attendance, with meeting the needs of the people, with renewing the lives of those who came. The next Sunday, the man appeared in his own church again, and when the pastor called for those who had anything to say, he stood up, still aglow with the events of the services and the presence of the Spirit. He said, "Preacher, I did go to that camp meeting. And the Word was preached with power. And the music was wonderful. The Holy Spirit was so present in that place that a mosquito bit me one night and went away singing, "There is Power in the Blood!" The pastor said, "Brother, you sit down and you shut up!" I admit that the fellow got pretty carried away with his feelings, but the language of the Spirit does glorify Christ, his cross, and his shed blood which brings redemption to our fallen lives.

The first gift of the Spirit, then, was a gift of speech — speech in different languages. The first act of the gift of speech was proclamation. You are never so likely to be filled with the Spirit as when you are witnessing to your faith in Christ. One of the marvelous results of the manifestation of the Spirit that day was that the disciples were filled with power; power for proclamation and praise. They told of "the mighty acts of God." The end result of the Spirit's descent upon those waiting people in the upper room was the birth of the church. The centripetal power, just opposite of the Tower of Babel again, of the Spirit was to gather, unite, and bring disciples and new believers into a community of faith with Christ (not self) at the center.

Death of a dream or the birth of the church? The dream was to glorify self, the Spirit was to glorify God. The dream died on the plain of Shinar. The promise became a glorious reality in the birth of the church. "To God be the Glory, Great Things He hath Done!"